THIS BOOK BELONGS TO

The Library of

....

Copyright @2023

Thank you for Purchasing my book and taking the time to read it from front to back. I am always grateful when a reader chooses my work and I hope you enjoyed it!

With the vast selection available online, I am touched that you chose to be purchasing my work and take valuable time out of your life to read it. My hope is that you feel you made the right decision.

I very much would like to know what you thought of the book. Please take the time to write an honest and informative review on Amazon.com. Your experience and opinions will be of great benefit to me and those readers looking to make an informed choice.

With much thanks.

Table of Contents

SUMMARY

Embracing the Kawaii Culture in Crochet:

A Delightful Journey into the World of Cute and Adorable Creations

Crochet, a versatile and beloved craft, has long been a means of creating beautiful and functional items. From cozy blankets to stylish garments, the possibilities are endless. However, in recent years, a new trend has emerged within the crochet community - the embrace of the kawaii culture.

Kawaii, a Japanese word meaning "cute" or "adorable," has become a global phenomenon, captivating people of all ages and backgrounds. It is characterized by its vibrant colors, whimsical designs, and charming characters. From Hello Kitty to Pikachu, kawaii has infiltrated various aspects of popular culture, including fashion, art, and even food.

In the world of crochet, kawaii has found its perfect match. The art of creating cute and lovable creatures, accessories, and decorations has become a delightful journey for crochet enthusiasts. By incorporating kawaii elements into their projects, crafters can infuse their creations with a sense of playfulness and joy.

One of the most appealing aspects of embracing the kawaii culture in crochet is the endless array of possibilities. From amigurumi, the Japanese art of crocheting small stuffed animals and dolls, to adorable accessories like keychains and hair clips, the options are truly limitless. Whether you're a beginner or an experienced crocheter, there is always a kawaii project waiting to be explored.

To get started on your kawaii crochet adventure, it's important to familiarize yourself with the key elements of this style. Bright and pastel colors are often used to create a cheerful and whimsical atmosphere. Soft and fluffy yarns, such as mohair or alpaca, can add an extra touch of cuteness to your creations. Additionally, incorporating small details like embroidered faces or tiny bows can bring your kawaii characters to life.

One of the most popular kawaii crochet projects is the amigurumi. These small, stuffed creatures are often inspired by animals, fruits, or even inanimate objects. With their round shapes, big eyes, and adorable expressions, amigurumi have a universal appeal that can bring a smile to anyone's face. From tiny bunnies to chubby pandas, the possibilities for amigurumi creations are truly endless.

The Joy of Crafting Amigurumi Crochet: The Joy of Crafting Amigurumi Crochet is a comprehensive guide that delves into the world of amigurumi crochet, a popular craft that involves creating adorable stuffed animals and characters using crochet techniques. This book is perfect for both beginners who are new to crochet and experienced crafters looking to expand their skills and create unique and personalized gifts.

The book starts off by introducing the basics of crochet, including the different types of yarn, hooks, and stitches used in amigurumi. It provides step-by-step instructions on how to create the basic crochet stitches, such as the chain stitch, single crochet, and double crochet, ensuring that even those with no prior crochet experience can follow along.

Once the reader has mastered the basic stitches, the book progresses to more advanced techniques, such as increasing and decreasing stitches, creating different shapes and textures, and adding embellishments to bring the amigurumi characters to life. The author provides clear and concise instructions, accompanied by detailed illustrations and photographs, making it easy for readers to understand and replicate the techniques.

One of the highlights of this book is the wide range of amigurumi patterns included. From cute animals like cats, dogs, and bunnies to whimsical characters like fairies, mermaids, and unicorns, there is something for everyone. Each pattern is accompanied by a list of materials needed, detailed instructions, and full-color photographs of the finished product, allowing readers to visualize the end result and choose their next project with confidence.

In addition to the patterns, the book also includes tips and tricks for customizing and personalizing the amigurumi creations. Readers are encouraged to experiment with different colors, yarns, and embellishments to make each project their own. The author also provides guidance on how to add facial features, such as eyes, noses, and mouths, as well as how to attach limbs and create unique poses for the amigurumi characters.

The Joy of Crafting Amigurumi Crochet goes beyond just providing patterns and instructions. It also explores the therapeutic benefits of crochet and the joy that comes from creating something with your own hands. The author shares personal anecdotes and stories from other crafters, highlighting the sense of accomplishment and satisfaction that can be gained from completing an amigurumi project.

Overall, The Joy of Crafting Amigurumi Crochet is a must-have book for anyone interested in amigurumi crochet.

What is Kawaii? Understanding the Aesthetics of Cuteness in Crochet: Kawaii, a Japanese term meaning "cute" or "adorable," has become a popular aesthetic in various forms of art and design, including crochet. This aesthetic is characterized by its emphasis on childlike innocence, simplicity, and charm. In the world of crochet, kawaii refers to the creation of cute and lovable items using yarn and a crochet hook.

The aesthetics of kawaii in crochet can be seen in the choice of colors, patterns, and designs. Pastel shades such as pink, baby blue, and mint green are commonly used to create a soft and gentle look. These colors evoke a sense of sweetness and playfulness, which are key elements of the kawaii aesthetic. Additionally, patterns featuring cute animals, flowers, and other whimsical motifs are often incorporated into kawaii crochet designs.

One of the defining characteristics of kawaii crochet is the use of amigurumi, which are small stuffed toys or dolls made using crochet techniques. Amigurumi are typically created using a single crochet stitch and are often worked in the round. These adorable creatures can take the form of animals, mythical creatures, or even inanimate objects, and are known for their large, expressive eyes and chubby proportions. The creation of amigurumi requires attention to detail and precision, as each stitch contributes to the overall cuteness of the finished piece.

In addition to amigurumi, kawaii crochet also includes other cute and charming items such as baby booties, hats, and blankets. These items are often adorned with bows, ribbons, and other decorative elements to enhance their cuteness. The use of soft and fluffy yarns, such as mohair or angora, further adds to the tactile appeal of kawaii crochet creations.

The appeal of kawaii crochet extends beyond its visual aesthetics. The act of creating these cute and lovable items can be a therapeutic and relaxing experience. The repetitive nature of crochet stitches, combined with the joy of seeing a project come to life, can provide a sense of accomplishment and satisfaction. Additionally, the act of gifting or displaying kawaii crochet creations can bring joy and happiness to both the creator and the recipient.

In conclusion, kawaii crochet is a delightful and enchanting aesthetic that brings the world of cuteness and charm to the realm of yarn and crochet. Through the use of pastel colors, whimsical patterns, and the creation of amigurumi and other cute items,...

The Basics of Amigurumi Crochet: Amigurumi crochet is a popular craft that involves creating small stuffed animals or dolls using crochet techniques. It originated in Japan and has gained popularity worldwide due to its cute and whimsical designs.

To get started with amigurumi crochet, you will need a few basic supplies. These include a crochet hook, yarn, stuffing, and a yarn needle. The crochet hook size will depend on the thickness of the yarn you are using, so it's important to choose the right size to achieve the desired result. The yarn can be any color or texture you prefer, as amigurumi allows for endless creativity and customization.

Once you have your supplies ready, it's time to learn the basic crochet stitches used in amigurumi. The most commonly used stitches are the single crochet (sc), double crochet (dc), and slip stitch (sl st). These stitches are used to create the body, limbs, and other parts of the amigurumi.

To start crocheting, you will need to make a slip knot and then create a foundation chain. The number of chains will depend on the size of the amigurumi you want to make. Once you have your foundation chain, you can start working in rounds or rows, depending on the pattern you are following.

When crocheting in rounds, you will need to join each round with a slip stitch and then start the next round. This creates a seamless and continuous piece, which is ideal for amigurumi. Crocheting in rows, on the other hand, creates a flat piece that can be sewn together later to form the amigurumi.

As you crochet, it's important to keep track of your stitches and rows to ensure that your amigurumi turns out the way you want it to. Using stitch markers or counting your stitches can help you stay organized and avoid any mistakes.

Once you have crocheted all the necessary pieces for your amigurumi, it's time to assemble them. This involves sewing the different parts together using a yarn needle and the same yarn you used for crocheting. You will also need to stuff the amigurumi with polyester fiberfill or any other stuffing material of your choice to give it a soft and cuddly feel.

After assembling and stuffing your amigurumi, you can add any additional details or embellishments to make it even more unique. This can include embroidering facial features, adding buttons or beads for eyes,..

"Materials and Tools for Kawaii Crochet: To create adorable and charming crochet projects in the kawaii style, you will need a variety of materials and tools. These will help you bring your cute and whimsical creations to life. Here is a detailed list of what you will need:

1. Yarn: Choose soft and vibrant colored yarns to give your kawaii crochet projects a lively and playful look. Opt for pastel shades or bright colors like pink, yellow, and mint green. Acrylic or cotton yarns work well for this style.

2. Crochet Hooks: Invest in a set of crochet hooks in various sizes to accommodate different yarn weights. The size of the hook will depend on the thickness of the yarn you are using. Generally, a 3.5mm or 4mm hook is suitable for most kawaii crochet projects.

3. Stuffing: To give your amigurumi (crocheted stuffed toys) their adorable shape, you will need stuffing material. Polyester fiberfill is commonly used for this purpose. Make sure to have enough on hand to fill your creations.

4. Safety Eyes: These are essential for adding a cute and expressive touch to your amigurumi. Safety eyes come in various sizes and colors, allowing you to customize the look of your creations. They are easy to attach and provide a professional finish.

5. Embroidery Floss: This is used for adding details and facial features to your kawaii crochet projects. Choose embroidery floss in colors that complement your yarn choices. Black and white are commonly used for eyes and mouth details.

6. Yarn Needle: A large-eyed yarn needle is necessary for weaving in loose ends and sewing pieces together. Look for a blunt-tipped needle to avoid splitting the yarn as you work.

7. Scissors: A good pair of sharp scissors is essential for cutting yarn and trimming excess threads. Keep them handy for any necessary snipping during your crochet process.

8. Stitch Markers: These are useful for marking specific stitches or rounds in your crochet pattern. They can be as simple as safety pins or specially designed markers. They help you keep track of your progress and ensure accuracy in your work.

9. Crochet Pattern Books or Online Resources: To get started with kawaii crochet, it's helpful to have access to crochet pattern books or online resources that specialize in this style. These resources will provide you with step-by-step instructions and inspiration for creating your own adorable designs.

Mastering the Magic Ring and Other Amigurumi Techniques: This book is a comprehensive guidebook that delves into the intricate art of creating amigurumi, a popular Japanese crochet technique used to make adorable stuffed toys and characters. This book is a must-have for both beginners and experienced crocheters who are looking to enhance their skills and expand their amigurumi repertoire.

The book starts off by introducing the magic ring technique, which is a fundamental skill in amigurumi. The author provides clear and concise instructions, accompanied by detailed illustrations, making it easy for readers to grasp this technique. The magic ring allows crocheters to create a tight and seamless starting point for their amigurumi projects, resulting in a more professional and polished finish.

Moving on from the magic ring, the book delves into various other amigurumi techniques that are essential for creating intricate and detailed designs. The author covers topics such as increasing and decreasing stitches, changing colors, and working in the round. Each technique is explained in a step-by-step manner, ensuring that readers can follow along and practice until they feel confident in their abilities.

One of the standout features of this book is the wide range of amigurumi patterns included. From cute animals to beloved characters from popular culture, there is something for everyone in this collection. Each pattern is accompanied by detailed instructions, a list of materials needed, and full-color photographs of the finished product. The author also provides helpful tips and tricks throughout the patterns, ensuring that readers can achieve the best results possible.

In addition to the patterns, the book also includes tips on choosing the right yarn and hooks for amigurumi projects, as well as guidance on stuffing and finishing techniques. The author shares her expertise and experience, offering valuable insights that will help readers create amigurumi toys that are not only visually appealing but also durable and long-lasting.

This book is not just a book, but a comprehensive resource that will inspire and empower crocheters to take their amigurumi skills to the next level. Whether you are a beginner looking to learn the basics or an experienced crocheter seeking new challenges, this book is sure to become an invaluable addition to your crafting library. With its clear instructions, detailed illustrations, and diverse range of patterns, this book is a must-have for anyone interested in the magical world of amigurumi.

Stitch Guide for Amigurumi Crochet: A comprehensive and detailed stitch guide for amigurumi crochet, providing step-by-step instructions and explanations for each stitch, along with helpful tips and techniques to enhance your crochet skills and create adorable amigurumi toys.

Amigurumi crochet has gained immense popularity in recent years, and for good reason. These cute and cuddly crocheted toys bring joy and delight to both children and adults alike. However, creating amigurumi requires a specific set of crochet stitches and techniques that may be unfamiliar to beginners or those new to the craft.

This stitch guide aims to bridge that gap by providing a thorough and easy-to-follow tutorial on the essential stitches used in amigurumi crochet. Whether you're a complete novice or an experienced crocheter looking to expand your skills, this guide will equip you with the knowledge and confidence to tackle any amigurumi project.

The guide begins with an introduction to the basic crochet stitches, such as the chain stitch, single crochet, double crochet, and slip stitch. Each stitch is explained in detail, with clear instructions and accompanying illustrations to ensure a thorough understanding. Additionally, common abbreviations used in crochet patterns are explained, allowing you to decipher and follow any amigurumi pattern with ease.

Moving on from the basics, the guide delves into more advanced stitches and techniques specific to amigurumi crochet. These include the magic ring, which is essential for creating a tight and seamless starting point for your amigurumi projects. The guide also covers increases and decreases, which are crucial for shaping your amigurumi toys and giving them their unique and adorable forms.

Furthermore, the guide explores various techniques for adding details and embellishments to your amigurumi creations. This includes surface crochet, which allows you to add decorative stitches and textures to your amigurumi toys. Additionally, the guide covers techniques for attaching limbs, embroidering facial features, and creating different types of hair and fur.

Throughout the guide, you'll find helpful tips and tricks to enhance your amigurumi crochet skills. These include suggestions for choosing the right yarn and hook size, as well as techniques for achieving consistent tension and avoiding common mistakes. The guide also provides guidance on reading amigurumi patterns, understanding gauge, and troubleshooting common issues that may arise during the crocheting process.

Reading Amigurumi Patterns and Charts: Reading Amigurumi Patterns and Charts is an essential skill for anyone interested in the art of crochet and creating adorable stuffed toys. Amigurumi, a Japanese term meaning "crocheted or knitted stuffed toy," has gained immense popularity in recent years due to its cute and whimsical nature.

To successfully create amigurumi toys, it is crucial to understand and interpret the patterns and charts provided. These patterns serve as a guide, outlining the steps and techniques required to complete the project. They typically include a list of materials needed, abbreviations used, and detailed instructions for each part of the toy.

One of the first things to familiarize yourself with when reading amigurumi patterns is the abbreviations. These abbreviations are commonly used in crochet patterns and are essential for understanding the instructions. Some common abbreviations include sc (single crochet), inc (increase), dec (decrease), and ch (chain). By understanding these abbreviations, you can easily follow the pattern and create the desired shape and structure of the amigurumi toy.

In addition to abbreviations, amigurumi patterns often include charts or diagrams. These charts provide a visual representation of the pattern, making it easier to understand the placement of stitches and the overall design. Charts are particularly helpful when working on complex patterns or when creating intricate details on the amigurumi toy. By referring to the chart, you can ensure that your stitches are placed correctly and that the toy turns out as intended.

When reading amigurumi patterns, it is important to pay attention to the specific instructions for each part of the toy. These instructions may include details on stitch counts, color changes, and shaping techniques. Following these instructions precisely will ensure that your amigurumi toy turns out as intended and that all the parts fit together seamlessly.

Furthermore, it is essential to have a good understanding of basic crochet techniques, such as single crochet, double crochet, and slip stitch. These techniques are often used in amigurumi patterns and are the building blocks for creating the various parts of the toy. By mastering these basic techniques, you will be able to confidently tackle more complex patterns and create amigurumi toys with ease.

In conclusion, reading amigurumi patterns and charts is a fundamental skill for anyone interested in creating these adorable stuffed toys. By understanding the abbreviations, referring to charts, and following the specific instructions, you can successfully bring these patterns to life.

Spheres, Cylinders, and Cones: The Building Blocks of Amigurumi: Amigurumi, the Japanese art of crocheting or knitting small stuffed animals or toys, relies heavily on three basic shapes: spheres, cylinders, and cones. These simple building blocks serve as the foundation for creating adorable and whimsical characters that bring joy to both children and adults alike.

The sphere, with its perfectly round shape, is a fundamental element in amigurumi. It forms the head, body, and limbs of many amigurumi creations. By using different sizes of spheres, one can easily create variations in the size and shape of the characters. The sphere is typically crocheted or knitted in continuous rounds, starting with a magic ring or a chain of stitches that is joined to form a circle. The number of stitches in each round is increased or decreased to achieve the desired size and shape.

Cylinders, on the other hand, are used to create the arms, legs, and torsos of amigurumi. They provide a more elongated and cylindrical shape compared to the spherical elements. Cylinders are created by crocheting or knitting in rows, back and forth, rather than in continuous rounds. This allows for the creation of straight edges and flat surfaces, which are essential for shaping the limbs and bodies of amigurumi characters. The number of rows and stitches can be adjusted to achieve the desired length and width of the cylinder.

Cones, with their tapered shape, are often used to create the noses, hats, and other pointed features of amigurumi. They add a playful and whimsical touch to the characters. Cones are created by starting with a small number of stitches at the tip and gradually increasing the number of stitches in each round or row. This creates a shape that narrows towards the top, resembling a cone. The size and length of the cone can be adjusted by varying the number of increases or decreases in each round or row.

By combining these three basic shapes, amigurumi artists can create an endless variety of characters and creatures. The possibilities are limited only by one's imagination. From cute animals like cats, dogs, and bears, to fantastical creatures like unicorns and dragons, the building blocks of spheres, cylinders, and cones provide a solid foundation for bringing these creations to life.

In addition to the basic shapes, amigurumi artists also utilize various techniques and stitches to add details and embellishments to their creations.

Creating Facial Features and Expressions of Amigurumi Crochet: Creating facial features and expressions for amigurumi crochet is an essential step in bringing these adorable crochet toys to life. The facial features and expressions play a crucial role in giving each amigurumi its unique personality and charm. Whether you are making a cute animal, a whimsical creature, or a beloved character, the facial features and expressions are what make them instantly recognizable and endearing.

To start creating the facial features, you will need a few basic materials such as yarn, a crochet hook, and stuffing. Additionally, you may also require safety eyes, embroidery floss, or buttons, depending on the design and style you want to achieve. Safety eyes are commonly used for amigurumi as they provide a professional and secure finish. However, if you prefer a more traditional or handmade look, you can opt for embroidery floss or buttons to create the eyes.

When it comes to the shape and size of the eyes, it largely depends on the desired expression and the size of your amigurumi. For a cute and innocent look, you can use round safety eyes or embroider small circles using embroidery floss. If you want to create a mischievous or playful expression, you can experiment with different eye shapes such as ovals or half-circles. The size of the eyes should be proportionate to the amigurumi's head, ensuring that they are not too big or too small.

Next, you can move on to creating the nose and mouth. For the nose, you can use a small piece of yarn or embroidery floss and sew it onto the face using a tapestry needle. The shape of the nose can vary depending on the animal or character you are creating. For example, a cat's nose can be a small triangle, while a bear's nose can be a round or oval shape. Similarly, the mouth can be created using embroidery floss or yarn, and you can experiment with different shapes such as a smile, a frown, or even a tongue sticking out.

To add more depth and dimension to the facial features, you can also incorporate blush or rosy cheeks. This can be achieved by using a small amount of blush powder or blush-colored yarn and lightly brushing or sewing it onto the cheeks. This subtle touch adds a touch of warmth and liveliness to the amigurumi's face.

Assembling and Stuffing Your Amigurumi Crochet: Assembling and stuffing your amigurumi crochet project is an essential step in bringing your creation to life. This process involves carefully joining the different crocheted pieces together and filling them with stuffing to give them shape and volume. By following a few simple techniques and tips, you can ensure that your amigurumi looks professional and well-crafted.

Firstly, before you begin assembling your amigurumi, it is important to weave in all loose ends and secure them tightly. This will prevent any unraveling or unsightly knots from appearing in your finished project. Use a yarn needle to carefully thread the loose ends through the stitches on the wrong side of the crocheted pieces, ensuring that they are hidden and secure.

Next, lay out all the crocheted pieces of your amigurumi project in the correct order according to the pattern instructions. This will help you visualize how the final product will look and ensure that you don't miss any important steps during the assembly process.

To join the crocheted pieces together, you can use a variety of techniques such as whip stitching, slip stitching, or single crochet stitches. The choice of joining method will depend on the specific pattern instructions and your personal preference. It is important to maintain an even tension while joining the pieces to ensure that the seams are neat and invisible.

When stuffing your amigurumi, it is crucial to use a high-quality stuffing material that is soft, resilient, and hypoallergenic. Polyester fiberfill is a popular choice among amigurumi enthusiasts as it provides excellent shape retention and is easily washable. Start by tearing small pieces of stuffing and carefully push them into the crocheted pieces using a stuffing tool or the end of a crochet hook. Be sure to distribute the stuffing evenly to avoid lumps or unevenness in your amigurumi.

As you stuff your amigurumi, periodically check the firmness and shape of the piece by gently squeezing it. You want the amigurumi to be firm enough to hold its shape but not overly stuffed, as this can distort the stitches and make the piece look bulky. Adjust the amount of stuffing accordingly until you achieve the desired firmness.

Once your amigurumi is fully assembled and stuffed, take the time to carefully shape and position any facial features or embellishments. This can be done using embroidery floss, safety eyes, or buttons, depending on the design.

Creating Your Own Kawaii Characters of Amigurumi Crochet: Creating your own kawaii characters of amigurumi crochet is a delightful and rewarding craft that allows you to bring your imagination to life. Amigurumi, a Japanese art form, involves creating small stuffed animals or characters using crochet techniques. The term "kawaii" refers to the Japanese concept of cuteness, which is often characterized by round shapes, big eyes, and adorable features. By combining these two elements, you can design and crochet your very own kawaii amigurumi characters that are unique and full of personality.

To begin creating your own kawaii characters, you will need some basic crochet skills and materials. Familiarize yourself with crochet stitches such as single crochet, double crochet, and slip stitch, as these will form the foundation of your amigurumi creations. Additionally, gather a selection of colorful yarns, crochet hooks in various sizes, stuffing material, and safety eyes or embroidery thread for the eyes.

Once you have your materials ready, it's time to let your creativity flow. Start by brainstorming ideas for your kawaii characters. Think about the animals or creatures that inspire you or bring you joy. Consider their unique characteristics and how you can incorporate them into your designs. For example, if you love cats, you could create a kawaii amigurumi cat with a round body, big eyes, and a cute little tail.

Next, sketch out your design on paper. This will help you visualize the shape and proportions of your character before you start crocheting. Pay attention to the details, such as the size and placement of the eyes, the shape of the ears or limbs, and any additional features like bows or accessories. Don't worry if your drawing skills aren't perfect – the purpose of the sketch is to serve as a guide for your crochet work.

Once you have your design sketched out, it's time to bring it to life with crochet. Start by creating a magic ring, which will serve as the starting point for your character's body. From there, follow a pattern or create your own by combining different crochet stitches to shape the body, head, and limbs. Remember to stuff your amigurumi as you go along to give it a soft and cuddly feel.

When it comes to adding the face to your kawaii character, you have a few options. Safety eyes are a popular choice as they give a professional and polished look to your amigurumi.

Fairy Tale and Folklore Inspired Amigurumi Crochet: Fairy Tale and Folklore Inspired Amigurumi Crochet is a unique and enchanting form of crochet that brings beloved characters and creatures from fairy tales and folklore to life. This art form combines the traditional craft of crochet with the whimsical and magical world of fairy tales, resulting in adorable and intricately designed amigurumi dolls and toys.

Amigurumi, a Japanese word meaning "crocheted or knitted stuffed toy," has gained immense popularity in recent years. It involves creating small, stuffed creatures using crochet techniques. These amigurumi dolls are known for their cute and cuddly appearance, making them perfect for children and adults alike.

What sets Fairy Tale and Folklore Inspired Amigurumi Crochet apart is its focus on characters and creatures from classic fairy tales and folklore. From the brave and beautiful princesses to the mischievous and cunning fairies, every character is meticulously crafted to capture their essence and charm.

Imagine holding a tiny Little Red Riding Hood doll, complete with her iconic red hooded cape and basket of goodies. Or how about a whimsical unicorn with a flowing mane and a magical horn? These amigurumi creations not only bring joy and nostalgia but also serve as a reminder of the timeless stories that have captivated our imaginations for generations.

The level of detail and craftsmanship in Fairy Tale and Folklore Inspired Amigurumi Crochet is truly remarkable. Each doll is carefully designed and crocheted using high-quality yarns and materials. The intricate patterns and stitches used bring out the unique characteristics of each character, making them instantly recognizable and endearing.

These amigurumi dolls are not just toys; they are works of art. They can be displayed as decorative pieces in a nursery or a child's room, adding a touch of whimsy and magic to the space. They also make for thoughtful and cherished gifts for both children and adults who appreciate the beauty and nostalgia of fairy tales and folklore.

Fairy Tale and Folklore Inspired Amigurumi Crochet is not limited to popular characters like Cinderella or Snow White. It also includes creatures from folklore, such as dragons, mermaids, and gnomes.

These mythical beings are brought to life through the skillful use of crochet techniques, resulting in unique and captivating amigurumi creations.

INTRODUCTION

Like so many, watching my grandmother crochet is my earliest memory of being intrigued by this beautiful fiber art. I received many lovely crochet gifts from her over the years, but sadly we lived too far apart for her to teach me. So one determined day (I was a teenager at this point) I decided that I would teach myself. I went to my local craft store and bought a book which promised I would learn how to crochet in 30 minutes! I was convinced! I bought the book, a skein of yarn, a crochet hook, and I was all set. Now you can imagine, it didn't go as smoothly as I had first imagined, but after some persevering, I made my first washcloth and found myself "hooked" and beginning my own crochet journey.

Creating my own patterns began when my daughter was born. I was a stay at home mom, and happy to be, but with a 15 month old and a newborn I found myself desperate for a creative outlet. Crochet became my therapy. During my babies' nap time I would design and create crocheted hats, blankets, and booties. If I thought it would look cute and they would like it, I made it! My kids have truly inspired all my crochet designs.

Moving forward a few years, my love of kawaii (cute) crochet began one summer morning after visiting the local farmer's market with my kids. After putting away all of the yummy fresh produce, I turned to see my kids creating their own farmer's market with play food. They played happily for hours, carefully setting it all up only to discover that they didn't quite have everything they needed. Of course, they proceeded to ask me for a lengthy list of fruits, veggies, and cakes. Now, when my kids ask me to make them something I find it impossible to say no, so I pulled out my favorite medium of yarn and busily began sketching and crocheting as fast as my fingers would allow.

I was already familiar with the kawaii faces that were appearing everywhere in retail stores, on social media, and in the cartoons my kids watched. These cute faces always bring a smile to my face, so I thought why not add a face to the apple I was making? Maybe my kids will love it even more, and you know what, they sure did!

Making seemingly everyday objects into crocheted kawaii has now became a passion of mine. It is my hope that the characters I have created bring a smile to your face and that this book encourages you as you take your own crochet journey. May we all discover a love for crochet, color, and all things cute!

Please refer to the Techniques section for guidance on any of the techniques used in this book.

SKILL LEVELS

The level of difficulty for each project is indicated by one of three faces, which are shown below for your reference. If you're new to crochet, start with a Beginner or Easy project. Alternatively, if you're looking for more of a challenge, go for an Intermediate project.

Beginner

Easy

Intermediate

Happy Crocheting!

TOOLS AND MATERIALS

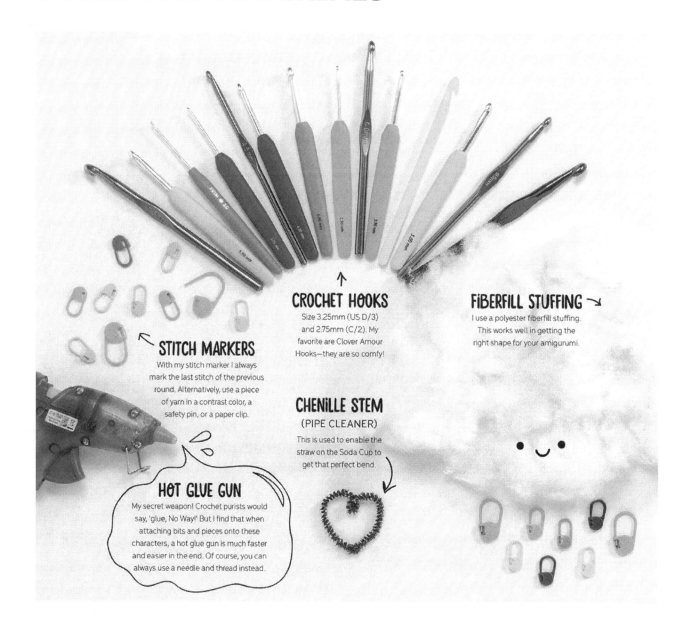

CROCHET HOOKS

Size 3.25mm (US D/3)
and 2.75mm (C/2). My
favorite are Clover Amour
Hooks—they are so comfy!

FIBERFILL STUFFING

I use a polyester fiberfill stuffing.
This works well in getting the
right shape for your amigurumi.

STITCH MARKERS

With my stitch marker I always
mark the last stitch of the previous
round. Alternatively, use a piece
of yarn in a contrast color, a
safety pin, or a paper clip.

CHENILLE STEM
(PIPE CLEANER)

This is used to enable the
straw on the Soda Cup to
get that perfect bend.

HOT GLUE GUN

My secret weapon! Crochet purists would
say, 'glue, No Way!' But I find that when
attaching bits and pieces onto these
characters, a hot glue gun is much faster
and easier in the end. Of course, you can
always use a needle and thread instead.

TOY SAFETY EYES

Black, sizes 5mm through 9mm is what I use the most. Alternatively, use black yarn to embroider the eyes (see Making Up: Inserting Safety Eyes).

SCISSORS

One of my favorite things to collect. They are best when they are pointy and sharp!

YARN NEEDLE

This is a blunt needle and is essentail for weaving in ends and shaping.

PINS

Used for holding parts together. I like to use T-Pins so that they don't get lost inside my amigurumi.

COTTON YARN

Two different yarn weights are used throughout this book and sometimes in the same pattern. Aran/Worsted Weight/4 ply and DK/Light Worsted/3 ply

WOODEN SKEWERS

The perfect tool to help you spread the fiberfill stuffing into every little corner. Plus they can be used instead of stuffing when something firmer is needed like in the Corn Dog crochet pattern.

COLOR THEORY

Color influences us in so many ways! I have always felt a love for color, but my fascination with it really began in college when I took a class on color theory. Learning how color affects us was eye opening, and from that point on I found myself paying more attention to how I felt around certain colors.

We are all drawn to different colors for different reasons, because it is personal and is the culmination of memories, experiences, and surroundings. Consequently, color plays such an important part in our lives and is the source of so much inspiration!

When choosing color for a crochet project, my best advice is to pay attention to colors you find yourself drawn to. This can be done while you go about your day; make a note of what catches your eye. Then collect these colors by taking a photo or by collecting samples of fabric, paint swatches, etc. You will begin to notice you gravitate toward certain colors.

If you love a particular color, but are not sure exactly how to use it in a color scheme, then think about where you see the hue in nature and emulate that. Nature makes it work every time! The chances are that the colors you are drawn to will all coordinate, but if you are like me and find yourself drawn to a huge range of color schemes, or perhaps you are wanting the fun and creative challenge of working with a color you are not naturally drawn to, then this is when a basic knowledge of color theory can be very helpful.

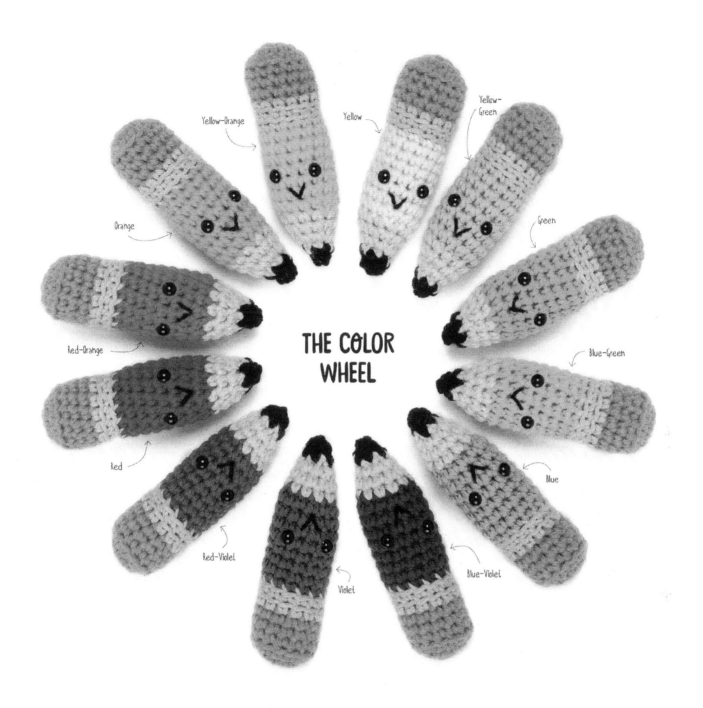

The Color Wheel

- Yellow-Orange
- Yellow
- Yellow-Green
- Orange
- Green
- Red-Orange
- Blue-Green
- Red
- Blue
- Red-Violet
- Blue-Violet
- Violet

COLOR TERMS

PRIMARY COLORS

The color wheel is made up of three primary colors that cannot be made from any other colors. They are Red, Yellow, and Blue.

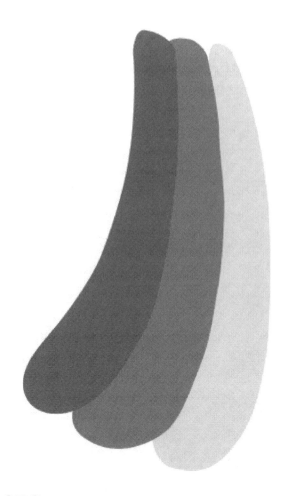

SECONDARY COLORS

These are Orange, Green, and Purple and are created by mixing two primary colors together.
Red + Yellow = Orange;
Yellow + Blue = Green;
Blue + Red = Purple.

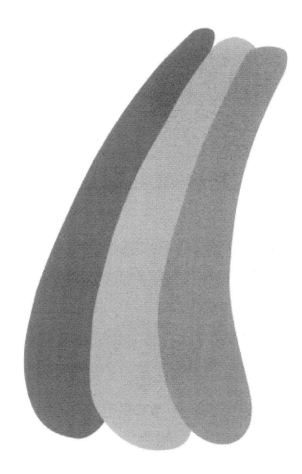

TERTIARY COLORS

These are created by mixing one primary and one secondary color together, and include blue-green, yellow-green, yellow-orange, red-orange, red-purple, and blue-purple.

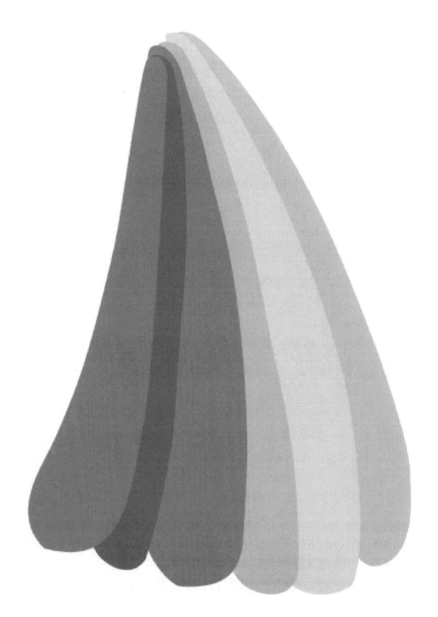

COMPLEMENTARY COLORS

These consist of any two colors which are directly opposite each other on the color wheel.

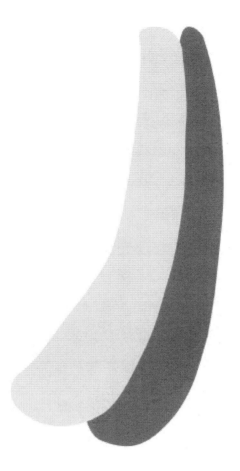

SPLIT-COMPLEMENTARY COLORS

These consist of any color on the wheel plus the two that flank its complement.

ANALAGOUS COLORS

These consist of any two to four colors which are side by side on the color wheel.

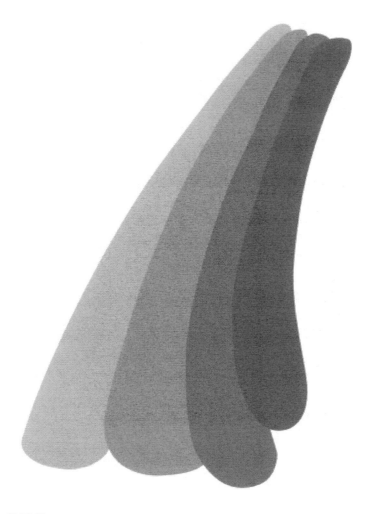

TRIADIC COLORS

These consist of any three colors evenly spaced around the color wheel.

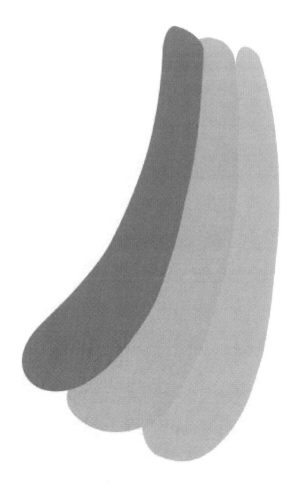

TETRADIC OR DOUBLE COMPLEMENTARY COLORS

These consist of four colors arranged into two complementary pairs.

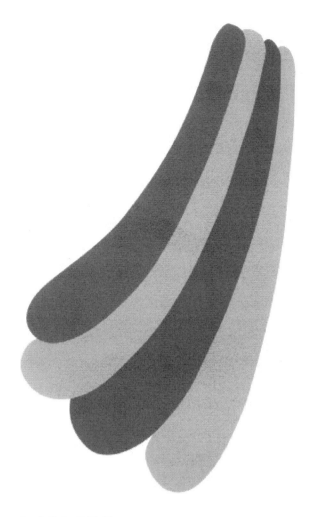

MONOCHROMATIC COLORS

These consist of one hue plus white, black, or grey to create tints, tones, and shades.

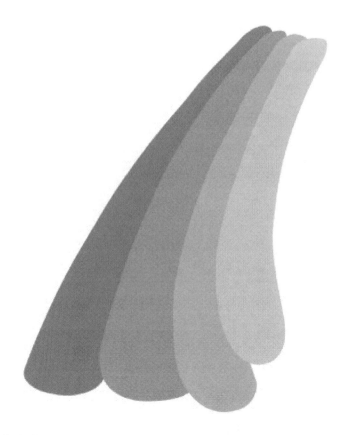

NEUTRAL COLORS

These consist of colors not associated with any single hue, like blacks, whites, and grays.

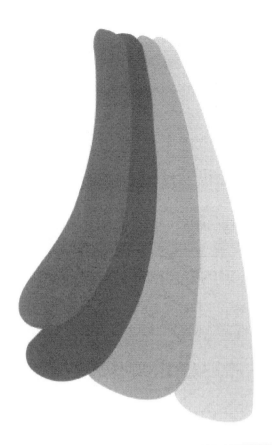

OTHER COLOR TERMS

HUE
The name of a color.

SATURATION
The intensity or purity of a hue.

VALUE
The degree of lightness or darkness of a hue.

SHADE
A hue produced by adding black.

TINT
A hue produced by adding white.

TONE
A hue produced by adding gray.

Red is the color of energy and excitement! It is vibrant, powerful, and full of passion. Red is strong-willed and can give us confidence. The color red can also stimulate the appetite and is associated with luck and prosperity.

APPLE

Materials

- 3.25mm (D/3) crochet hook
- Paintbox Yarns Cotton Aran yarn: one 50g (1.75oz) ball each of Pillar Red (**red**), Coffee Bean (**brown**), and Grass Green (**green**)
- 8mm safety eyes

- Scraps of **orange** and **black** yarn
- Fiberfill stuffing
- Yarn needle
- Stitch marker

Finished Size

9cm (3$\frac{1}{2}$in) tall by 9cm (3$\frac{1}{2}$in) wide

Gauge

5 sc sts and 6 rows = 2.5cm (1in)

APPLE

Rnd 1: with **red** yarn, sc 8 in magic loop [8]

Rnd 2: sc in each st around [8]

Rnd 3: (sc 1, 2 sc in next st) 4 times [12]

Rnd 4: sc in each st around [12]

Rnd 5: (sc 1, 2 sc in next st) 6 times [18]

Rnd 6: (sc 2, 2 sc in next st) 6 times [24]

Rnd 7: (sc 3, 2 sc in next st) 6 times [30]

Rnd 8: (sc 4, 2 sc in next st) 6 times [36]

Rnd 9: (sc 5, 2 sc in next st) 6 times [42]

Rnd 10: (sc 6, 2 sc in next st) 6 times [48]

Rnd 11: (sc 7, 2 sc in next st) 6 times [54]

Rnds 12–16: sc in each st around [54]

Rnd 17: (sc 25, sc2tog) twice [52]

Rnd 18: sc in each st around [52]

Rnd 19: (sc 11, sc2tog) 4 times [48]

Rnd 20: sc in each st around [48]

Rnd 21: (sc 10, sc2tog) 4 times [44]

Rnd 22: (sc 9, sc2tog) 4 times [40]

Rnd 23: (sc 8, sc2tog) 4 times [36]

Attach the stem and leaf to the top of the apple. Place 8mm safety eyes between **Rnds 16 and 17** with 5 sts in between. Begin to stuff with fiberfill.

Rnd 24: (sc 4, sc2tog) 6 times [30]

Rnd 25: (sc 3, sc2tog) 6 times [24]

Rnd 26: (sc 2, sc2tog) 6 times [18]

Rnd 27: sc in each st around [18]

Rnd 28: (sc2tog) 9 times [9]

Finish stuffing. Fasten off and leave a long yarn tail.

With a yarn needle, weave the tail through FLO to close the opening.

Begin shaping by inserting the needle from the center bottom to the center top. Insert the needle back down from slightly off the center top to slightly off the center bottom. Pull the yarn to create an indentation in the top of the apple.

Insert the needle from the center bottom to the center top. Pull to create an indentation in the bottom of the apple. Finish off and weave in all ends.

Add stitches for the mouth and cheeks using **black** and **orange** yarn (see Making Up: Stitching Facial Details).

LEAF

With **green** yarn, ch 10.

Rnd 1: sl st in 2nd ch from hook, sc 1, hdc 1, dc 4, hdc 1, sc 3 in last st, working on the other side of the foundation ch, hdc 1, dc 4, hdc 1, sc 1, sl st 1, sl st in beginning skipped ch st.

Invisible fasten off (see Finishing: Invisible Fasten Off) and weave in all ends. Attach to the top of the apple.

Leaf Chart

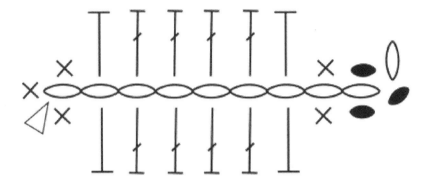

STEM

With 2 strands of **brown** yarn, ch 9.

Row 1: working in back bump loops (see Special Stitches: Back Bump), sc in 2nd ch from hook, sl st 7.

Fasten off and weave in all ends. Attach to the top of the apple.

AN APPLE A DAY...

Model your creation on your favorite type of apple, whether it's a bright green Granny Smith, a sweet Gala, a pretty Pink Lady or a Red Delicious.

CHRISTMAS LIGHT

Materials

- 3.25mm (D/3) crochet hook
- Paintbox Yarns Cotton Aran yarn: one 50g (1.75oz) ball each of Pillar Red (**red**) and Grass Green (**green**)
- 6mm safety eyes

- Scraps of **orange** and **black** yarn
- Fiberfill stuffing
- Yarn needle
- Stitch marker

Finished Size

10cm (4in) tall by 5cm (2in) wide

Gauge

5 sc sts and 6 rows = 2.5cm (1in)

CHRISTMAS LIGHT

Rnd 1: with **red** yarn, sc 6 in magic loop [6]

Rnd 2: sc in each st around [6]

Rnd 3: (sc 1, 2 sc in next st) 3 times [9]

Rnd 4: (sc 2, 2 sc in next st) 3 times [12]

Rnd 5: (sc 3, 2 sc in next st) 3 times [15]

Rnd 6: (sc 4, 2 sc in next st) 3 times [18]

Rnd 7: (sc 5, 2 sc in next st) 3 times [21]

Rnd 8: (sc 6, 2 sc in next st) 3 times [24]

Rnd 9: (sc 3, 2 sc in next st) 6 times [30]

Rnds 10-14: sc in each st around [30]

Place 6mm safety eyes between **Rnds 9 and 10** with 3 sts in between. Begin to stuff with fiberfill.

Rnd 15: (sc 3, sc2tog) 6 times [24]

Rnd 16: (sc 2, sc2tog) 6 times [18]

Rnd 17: sc in each st around [18]

Rnd 18: (sc 1, sc2tog) 6 times [12]

Rnd 19: change to **green** yarn, sc in each st around [12]

Rnds 20-21: sc in each st around [12]

Rnd 22: working in BLO, (sc2tog) 6 times [6]

Finish stuffing. Fasten off and leave a long yarn tail.

With a yarn needle, weave the tail through FLO to close the opening. Weave in all ends.

Add stitches for the mouth and cheeks using **black** and **orange** yarn (see Making Up: Stitching Facial Details).

CHILI PEPPER

Materials

- 3.25mm (D/3) crochet hook
- Paintbox Yarns Cotton Aran yarn: one 50g (1.75oz) ball each of Pillar Red (**red**) and Grass Green (**green**)
- 6mm safety eyes
- Scraps of **orange** and **black** yarn
- Fiberfill stuffing
- Yarn needle
- Stitch marker

Finished Size

13cm (5in) tall by 4cm ($1^1/_2$in) wide

Gauge

5 sc sts and 6 rows = 2.5cm (1in)

CHILI PEPPER

Rnd 1: with **red** yarn, sc 6 in magic loop [6]

Rnd 2: 2 sc in each st around [12]

Rnd 3: sc in each st around [12]

Rnd 4: (sc 1, 2 sc in next st) 6 times [18]

Rnd 5: (sc 2, 2 sc in next st) 6 times [24]

Rnds 6-7: sc in each st around [24]

Rnd 8: (sc 2, sc2tog) 6 times [18]

Rnds 9-11: sc in each st around [18]

Place 6mm safety eyes between **Rnds 6 and 7** with 3 sts in between. Begin to stuff with fiberfill.

Rnd 12: sc 4, sc2tog, sc 12 [17]

Rnd 13: sc 4, sc2tog, sc 11 [16]

Rnd 14: sc 4, sc2tog, sc 10 [15]

Rnd 15: sc 4, sc2tog, sc 9 [14]

Rnd 16: sc 4, sc2tog, sc 8 [13]

Rnd 17: sc 4, sc2tog, sc 7 [12]

Rnd 18: sc 4, sc2tog, sc 6 [11]

Rnd 19: sc 4, sc2tog, sc 5 [10]

Rnd 20: sc 4, sc2tog, sc 4 [9]

Rnd 21: sc 4, sc2tog, sc 3 [8]

Rnd 22: sc 4, sc2tog, sc 2 [7]

Rnd 23: sc 4, sc2tog, sc 1 [6]

Finish stuffing. Fasten off and leave a long yarn tail.

With a yarn needle, weave the tail through FLO to close the opening. Weave in all ends.

Add stitches for the mouth and cheeks using **black** and **orange** yarn (see Making Up: Stitching Facial Details).

CAP

Rnd 1: with **green** yarn sc 6 in magic loop [6]

Rnd 2: 2 sc in each st around [12]

Rnd 3: (sc 1, 2 sc in next st) 6 times [18]

Rnd 4: sc in each st around [18]

Invisible fasten off (see Finishing: Invisible Fasten Off) and weave in all ends. Attach to the top of the chili pepper.

STEM

With **green** yarn, ch 7.

Rnd 1: working in back bump loops (see Special Stitches: Back Bump), sc in 2nd ch from hook, sl st 5 [6]

Fasten off, attach to the top center of the cap, and weave in the ends.

POPCORN

Materials

- 2.75mm (C/2) and 3.25mm (D/3) crochet hooks
- Paintbox Yarns Cotton Aran yarn: one 50g (1.75oz) ball each of Pillar Red (**red**), Paper White (**white**), and Banana Cream (**cream**)
- Paintbox Yarns Cotton DK yarn: one 50g (1.75oz) ball each of Banana Cream (**cream**) and Daffodil Yellow (**yellow**)
- 8mm safety eyes
- Scraps of **white** and **black** yarn
- Fiberfill stuffing
- Yarn needle
- Stitch marker

Finished Size

13cm (5in) tall by 10cm (4in) wide

Gauge

5 sc sts and 6 rows = 2.5cm (1in) using Aran yarn

6 sc sts and 7 rows = 2.5cm (1in) using DK yarn

TOP SECTION OF BUCKET

Rnd 1: with **3.25mm** hook and **cream Aran** yarn, sc 6 in magic loop [6]

Rnd 2: 2 sc in each st around [12]

Rnd 3: (sc 1, 2 sc in next st) 6 times [18]

Rnd 4: (sc 2, 2 sc in next st) 6 times [24]

Rnd 5: (sc 3, 2 sc in next st) 6 times [30]

Rnd 6: (sc 4, 2 sc in next st) 6 times [36]

Rnd 7: (sc 5, 2 sc in next st) 6 times [42]

Rnd 8: (sc 6, 2 sc in next st) 6 times [48]

Rnd 9: (sc 7, 2 sc in next st) 6 times [54]

Invisible fasten off (see Finishing: Invisible Fasten Off) and weave in all ends.

POPCORN BUCKET

Rnd 1: with **3.25mm** hook and **red** yarn, sc 6 in magic loop [6]

Rnd 2: 2 sc in each st around [12]

Rnd 3: (sc 1, 2 sc in next st) 6 times [18]

Rnd 4: (sc 2, 2 sc in next st) 6 times [24]

Rnd 5: (sc 3, 2 sc in next st) 6 times [30]

Rnd 6: (sc 4, 2 sc in next st) 6 times [36]

Rnd 7: (sc 5, 2 sc in next st) 6 times [42]

Rnd 8: working in BLO, sc in each st around [42]

Rnds 9-11: sc in each st around [42]

Rnd 12: (sc 6, 2 sc in next st) 6 times [48]

Rnds 13-15: sc in each st around [48]

Rnd 16: (sc 7, 2 sc in next st) 6 times [54]

Rnds 17-19: sc in each st around [54]

Place 8mm safety eyes between **Rnds 14 and 15** with 5 sts in between. Begin to stuff with fiberfill.

Rnd 20: (sc 8, 2 sc in next st) 6 times [60]

Rnd 21: place the top piece in the bucket and line up the stitches from **Rnd 19** of the bucket and **Rnd 9** of the top section. With the same **red** yarn used to make the bucket, sc around working in both loops of both pieces to join them together (see Making Up: Crocheting Two Pieces Together), sl st in first sc to join [60]

Rnd 22: ch 1, (sc 8, sc2tog) 6 times, sl st in first sc to join [54]

Rnd 23: change to **white** yarn, ch 1, sc in each st around, sl st in first sc to join [54]

Rnd 24: sl st in each st around [54]

Invisible fasten off and weave in all ends. Add stitches for the mouth and cheeks using **black** and **white** yarn (see Making Up: Stitching Facial Details).

POPCORN

Rnd 1: with **2.75mm** hook and **cream DK** yarn, sc 5 in magic loop [5]

Rnd 2: 2 sc in each st around [10]

Rnd 3: (sc 1, 2 sc in next st) 5 times [15]

Rnd 4: (sc2tog, sc 1) 5 times [10]

Rnd 5: (sc2tog) 5 times [5]

Rnd 6: working in FLO throughout, (work sl st 1 + ch 2 + 3-dc-bl (see Special Stitches: 3-Double Crochet Bobble) + ch 2 + sl st all in same st) 4 times, sl st in last st.

Stuff with fiberfill. Fasten off and leave a long yarn tail. With a yarn needle weave the tail through BLO from **Rnd 5** to close the opening, weave in the ends.

Make a total of 21 pieces of popcorn, 14 in **cream** DK and 7 in **yellow** DK. Attach the popcorn to the top section of the bucket.

SODA CUP

Materials

- 3.25mm (D/3) crochet hook
- Paintbox Yarns Cotton Aran yarn: one 50g (1.75oz) ball each of Pillar Red (**red**), Coffee Bean (**brown**), and Paper White (**white**)
- 8mm safety eyes
- Scraps of **orange** and **black** yarn
- Fiberfill stuffing
- Chenille stem (pipe cleaner)
- Yarn needle
- Stitch marker

Finished Size

18cm (7in) tall by 10cm (4in) wide

Gauge

5 sc sts and 6 rows = 2.5cm (1in)

CUP

Rnd 1: with **red** yarn, sc 6 in magic loop [6]

Rnd 2: 2 sc in each st around [12]

Rnd 3: (sc 1, 2 sc in next st) 6 times [18]

Rnd 4: (sc 2, 2 sc in next st) 6 times [24]

Rnd 5: (sc 3, 2 sc in next st) 6 times [30]

Rnd 6: working in BLO, sc in each st around [30]

Rnds 7-11: sc in each st around [30]

Rnd 12: (sc 4, 2 sc in next st) 6 times [36]

Rnds 13-16: sc in each st around [36]

Rnd 17: (sc 5, 2 sc in next st) 6 times [42]

Rnds 18-21: sc in each st around [42]

Rnd 22: (sc 6, 2 sc in next st) 6 times [48]

Rnds 23-26: sc in each st around [48]

Place 8mm safety eyes between **Rnds 16 and 17** with 5 sts in between. Begin to stuff with fiberfill.

Rnd 27: (sc 7, 2 sc in next st) 6 times [54]

Rnd 28: sc in each st around [54]

Do not finish off or cut the yarn. Finish stuffing. Make the Soda before moving on to **Rnd 29**.

Rnd 29: Place the soda in the cup and line up the stitches from **Rnd 28** of the cup and **Rnd 9** of the soda. With the yarn used to make the cup, sc in each st around working in both loops of both pieces to join them together (see Making Up: Crocheting Two Pieces Together) [54]

Rnd 30: ch 1, (sc 7, sc2tog) 6 times, join with sl st in first st [48]

Rnd 31: sl st in each st around [48]

Invisible fasten off (see Finishing: Invisible Fasten Off) and weave in all ends. Add stitches for the mouth and cheeks using **black** and **orange** yarn (see Making Up: Stitching Facial Details).

Begin shaping by inserting needle from center bottom to center top, insert needle back down from center top to slightly off center bottom. Insert needle from center bottom to center top. Pull to create an indentation in the bottom of the soda. Finish off and weave in the ends.

SODA

Rnd 1: with **brown** yarn, sc 6 in magic loop [6]

Rnd 2: 2 sc in each st around [12]

Rnd 3: (sc 1, 2 sc in next st) 6 times [18]

Rnd 4: (sc 2, 2 sc in next st) 6 times [24]

Rnd 5: (sc 3, 2 sc in next st) 6 times [30]

Rnd 6: (sc 4, 2 sc in next st) 6 times [36]

Rnd 7: (sc 5, 2 sc in next st) 6 times [42]

Rnd 8: (sc 6, 2 sc in next st) 6 times [48]

Rnd 9: (sc 7, 2 sc in next st) 6 times [54]

Invisible fasten off and weave in the ends.

LID

Rnd 1: with **white** yarn, sc 6 in magic loop [6]

Rnd 2: 2 sc in each st around [12]

Rnd 3: (sc 1, 2 sc in next st) 6 times [18]

Rnd 4: (sc 2, 2 sc in next st) 6 times [24]

Rnd 5: (sc 3, 2 sc in next st) 6 times [30]

Rnd 6: (sc 4, 2 sc in next st) 6 times [36]

Rnd 7: (sc 5, 2 sc in next st) 6 times [42]

Rnd 8: (sc 6, 2 sc in next st) 6 times [48]

Rnd 9: (sc 7, 2 sc in next st) 6 times [54]

Rnd 10: (sc 8, 2 sc in next st) 6 times [60]

Rnd 11: working in BLO, sc in each st around [60]

Rnd 12: sc in each st around [60]

Rnd 13: sl st in each st around [60]

Invisible fasten off and weave in the ends.

STRAW

Rnd 1: with **red** yarn, sc 5 in magic loop [5]

Rnds 2-14: sc in each st around [5]

Insert a chenille stem and bend to form the straw.

Fasten off and leave a long yarn tail. With a yarn needle, weave the tail through FLO to close the opening. Using the BLO, sew straw to the top center of the lid.

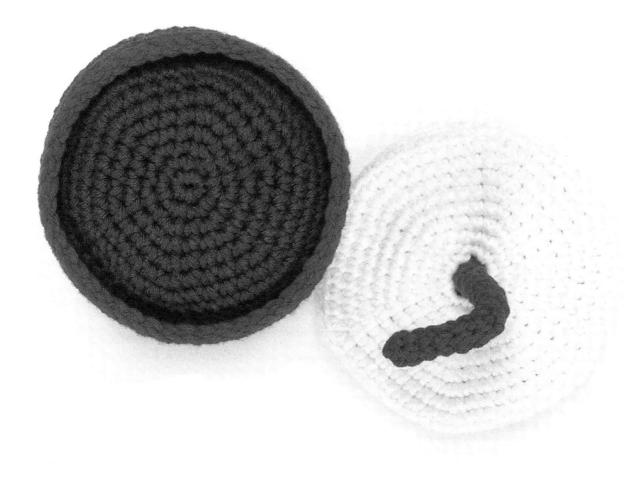

Orange is intellectual and full of
adventure. It is associated with warmth,
health, optimism, and energy. Orange
can offer emotional strength in difficult
times and motivate us to look on the
bright side of life.

CARROT CAKE

Materials

- 2.75mm (C/2) and 3.25mm (D/3) crochet hooks
- Paintbox Yarns Cotton Aran yarn: one 50g (1.75oz) ball each of Soft Fudge (**brown**) and Vanilla Cream (**cream**)
- Paintbox Yarns Cotton DK yarn: one 50g (1.75oz) ball each of Grass Green (**green**) and Mandarin Orange (**orange**)
- 7mm safety eyes
- Scraps of **orange** and **black** yarn
- Fiberfill stuffing
- Yarn needle
- Stitch marker

Finished Size

11.5cm (4^1/$_2$in) tall by 7.5cm (3in) wide

Gauge

5 sc sts and 6 rows = 2.5cm (1in) using Aran yarn

6 sc sts and 7 rows = 2.5cm (1in) using DK yarn

CAKE

Beginning at the top of the cake:

Rnd 1: with **3.25mm** hook and **cream** yarn, sc 6 in magic loop [6]

Rnd 2: 2 sc in each st around [12]

Rnd 3: (sc 1, 2 sc in next st) 6 times [18]

Rnd 4: (sc 2, 2 sc in next st) 6 times [24]

Rnd 5: (sc 3, 2 sc in next st) 6 times [30]

Rnd 6: (sc 4, 2 sc in next st) 6 times [36]

Rnd 7: (sc 5, 2 sc in next st) 6 times [42]

Rnd 8: working in BLO, sc in each st around [42]

Rnd 9: change to **brown** yarn, sc in each st around [42]

Rnds 10-11: sc in each st around [42]

Rnd 12: change to **cream** yarn, sc in each st around [42]

Rnd 13: change to **brown** yarn, sc in each st around [42]

Rnds 14-15: sc in each st around [42]

Rnd 16: change to **cream** yarn, sc in each st around [42]

Rnd 17: change to **brown** yarn, sc in each st around [42]

Rnds 18-19: sc in each st around [42]

Place 7mm safety eyes between **Rnds 12 and 13** with 4 sts in between. Begin to stuff with fiberfill.

Rnd 20: working in BLO, (sc 5, sc2tog) 6 times [36]

Rnd 21: (sc 4, sc2tog) 6 times [30]

Rnd 22: (sc 3, sc2tog) 6 times [24]

Rnd 23: (sc 2, sc2tog) 6 times [18]

Rnd 24: (sc 1, sc2tog) 6 times [12]

Rnd 25: (sc2tog) 6 times [6]

Finish stuffing. Fasten off and leave a long yarn tail. With a yarn needle, weave the tail through FLO to close the opening.

Begin shaping by inserting the needle from the center bottom to the center top. Insert the needle back down from center top to slightly off the center bottom. Insert needle from center bottom to center top. Pull to create an indentation in the bottom of the cake. Fasten off and weave in the ends.

With the **cream** edge of the cake at the top, add stitches for the mouth and cheeks using **black** and **orange** yarn (see Making Up: Stitching Facial Details).

FROSTING

Row 1: with **3.25mm** hook and **cream** yarn (ch 4, 5-dc-bl (see Special Stitches: 5-Double Crochet Bobble) in 4th ch from hook) 12 times, ch 1 [12 bobble sts]

Fasten off and weave in all ends. Attach to the top edge of the cake.

CARROT STEM (MAKE 6)

With **2.75mm** hook and **green** yarn, ch 10.

Row 1: sc in 2nd ch from hook, sc 8 [9]

Fasten off and weave in the ends. Attach two stems to the top of each carrot.

CARROT (MAKE 3)

Rnd 1: with **2.75mm** hook and **orange** yarn sc 6 in magic loop [6]

Rnd 2: 2 sc in each st around [12]

Rnd 3: (sc 1, 2 sc in next st) 6 times [18]

Rnds 4-5: sc in each st around [18]

Rnd 6: (sc 4, sc2tog) 3 times [15]

Rnd 7: sc in each st around [15]

Rnd 8: (sc 3, sc2tog) 3 times [12]

Rnd 9: sc in each st around [12]

Rnd 10: working in BLO, (sc2tog) 6 times [6]

Stuff with fiberfill. Fasten off and leave a long yarn tail. With a yarn needle weave the tail through FLO to close the opening, weave in the ends.

Attach the carrots to the top of the cake.

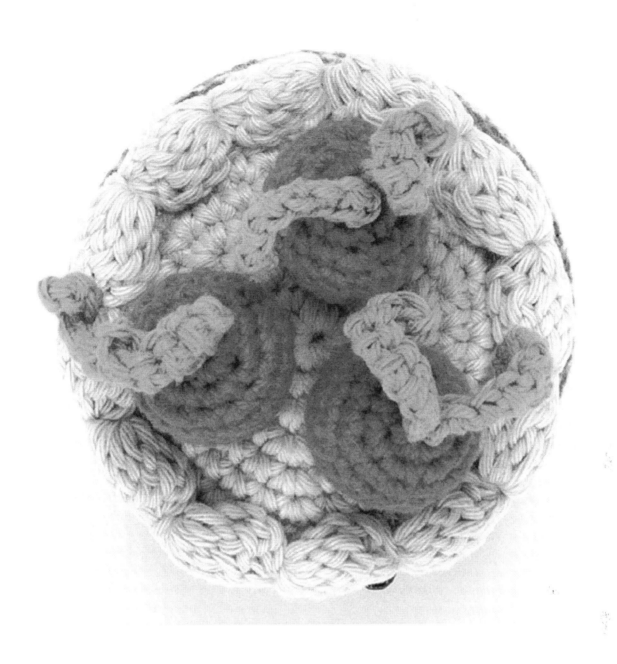

CREAMSICLE

Materials

- 2.75mm (C/2) crochet hook
- Paintbox Yarns Cotton DK yarn: one 50g (1.75oz) ball each of Mandarin Orange (**orange**), Paper White (**white**), and Light Caramel (**tan**)
- 7mm safety eyes
- Scraps of **dark orange** and **black** yarn
- Fiberfill stuffing
- Yarn needle
- Stitch marker

Finished Size

14cm (5$\frac{1}{2}$in) tall by 5cm (2in) wide

Gauge

6 sc sts and 7 rows = 2.5cm (1in)

CREAMSICLE

With **orange** yarn, ch 7.

Rnd 1: 2 sc in 2nd ch from hook, sc 4, 4 sc in last st, working on the other side of the foundation ch, sc 4, 2 sc in last st [16]

Rnd 2: 2 sc in next 2 sts, sc 5, 2 sc in next 3 sts, sc 5, 2 sc in last st [22]

Rnd 3: 2 sc in next 3 sts, sc 7, 2 sc in next 4 sts, sc 7, 2 sc in last st [30]

Rnds 4-24: sc in each st around [30]

Rnd 25: change to **white** yarn, sc in each st around [30]

Rnds 26-27: sc in each st around [30]

Place 7mm safety eyes between **Rnds 18 and 19** with 4 sts in between. Begin to stuff with fiberfill.

Rnd 28: working in BLO, (sc2tog) 4 times, sc 7, (sc2tog) 4 times, sc 7 [22]

Rnd 29: (sc2tog) 3 times, sc 5, (sc2tog) 3 times, sc 5 [16]

Rnd 30: change to **tan** yarn, (sc2tog) twice, sc 2, (sc2tog) 3 times, sc 2, sc2tog [10]

Rnds 31-39: sc in each st around [10]

Finish stuffing. Fasten off and leave a long yarn tail. With a yarn needle, weave the tail through FLO to close the opening. Weave in the ends.

Add stitches for the mouth and cheeks using **black** and **dark orange** yarn (see Making Up: Stitching Facial Details).

ORANGE

Materials

- 3.25mm (D/3) crochet hook
- Paintbox Yarns Cotton Aran yarn: one 50g (1.75oz) ball each of Mandarin Orange (**orange**) and Grass Green (**green**)
- 7mm safety eyes
- Scraps of **red** and **black** yarn
- Fiberfill stuffing
- Yarn needle
- Stitch marker

Finished Size

9cm (3$\frac{1}{2}$in) tall by 9cm (3$\frac{1}{2}$in) wide

Gauge

5 sc sts and 6 rows = 2.5cm (1in)

ORANGE

Rnd 1: with **green** yarn, sc 6 in magic loop [6]

Rnd 2: change to **orange** yarn, 2 sc in each st around [12]

Rnd 3: (sc 1, 2 sc in next st) 6 times [18]

Rnd 4: (sc 2, 2 sc in next st) 6 times [24]

Rnd 5: (sc 3, 2 sc in next st) 6 times [30]

Rnd 6: (sc 4, 2 sc in next st) 6 times [36]

Rnd 7: sc in each st around [36]

Rnd 8: (sc 5, 2 sc in next st) 6 times [42]

Rnd 9: sc in each st around [42]

Rnd 10: (sc 6, 2 sc in next st) 6 times [48]

Rnd 11: sc in each st around [48]

Rnd 12: (sc 7, 2 sc in next st) 6 times [54]

Rnd 13: sc in each st around [54]

Rnd 14: (sc 7, sc2tog) 6 times [48]

Rnds 15-16: sc in each st around [48]

Rnd 17: (sc 6, sc2tog) 6 times [42]

Rnds 18-19: sc in each st around [42]

Place 7mm safety eyes between **Rnds 13 and 14** with 5 sts in between. Begin to stuff with fiberfill.

Rnd 20: (sc 5, sc2tog) 6 times [36]

Rnd 21: (sc 4, sc2tog) 6 times [30]

Rnd 22: (sc 3, sc2tog) 6 times [24]

Rnd 23: (sc 2, sc2tog) 6 times [18]

Rnd 24: (sc 1, sc2tog) 6 times [12]

Rnd 25: (sc2tog) 6 times [6]

Finish stuffing. Fasten off and leave a long yarn tail. With a yarn needle, weave the tail through FLO to close the opening. Weave in all ends.

Add stitches for the mouth and cheeks using **black** and **red** yarn (see Making Up: Stitching Facial Details).

LEAF (MAKE 2)

With **green** yarn, ch 10.

Rnd 1: sl st in 2nd ch from hook, sc 1, hdc 1, dc 4, hdc 1, sc 3 in last st, working on the other side of the foundation ch, hdc 1, dc 4, hdc 1, sc 1, sl st 1, sl st in beginning skipped ch st.

Invisible fasten off (see Finishing: Invisible Fasten Off) and weave in all ends. Attach to the top of the orange.

Leaf Chart

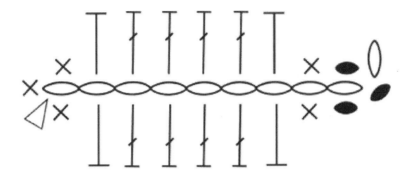

ORANGE JUICE

Materials

- 2.75mm (C/2) crochet hook
- Paintbox Yarns Cotton DK yarn: one 50g (1.75oz) ball each of Mandarin Orange (**orange**), Misty Grey (**gray**), and Paper White (**white**)
- 7mm safety eyes
- Scraps of **red** and **black** yarn
- Fiberfill stuffing
- Yarn needle
- Stitch marker

Finished Size

14cm (5^1/$_2$in) tall by 7.5cm (3in) wide

Gauge

6 sc sts and 7 rows = 2.5cm (1in)

CUP

Rnd 1: with **gray** yarn, sc 6 in magic loop [6]

Rnd 2: 2 sc in each st around [12]

Rnd 3: (sc 1, 2 sc in next st) 6 times [18]

Rnd 4: (sc 2, 2 sc in next st) 6 times [24]

Rnd 5: (sc 3, 2 sc in next st) 6 times [30]

Rnd 6: (sc 4, 2 sc in next st) 6 times [36]

Rnd 7: (sc 5, 2 sc in next st) 6 times [42]

Rnd 8: working in BLO, sc in each st around [42]

Rnd 9: sc in each st around [42]

Rnd 10: change to **orange** yarn, sc in each st around [42]

Rnds 11-13: sc in each st around [42]

Rnd 14: (sc 6, 2 sc in next st) 6 times [48]

Rnds 15-29: sc in each st around [48]

Place 7mm safety eyes between **Rnds 17 and 18** with 5 sts in between. Begin to stuff with fiberfill.

Rnd 30: (sc 7, 2 sc in next st) 6 times [54]

Rnd 31: sc in each st around [54]

Invisible fasten off (see Finishing: Invisible Fasten Off) and weave in all ends. Make the Juice before moving on to **Rnd 32**. Finish stuffing.

Rnd 32: Place the juice in the cup and line up the stitches from **Rnd 31** of the cup and **Rnd 9** of the juice. With **gray** yarn, sc in each st around working in both loops of both pieces to join them together (see Making Up: Crocheting Two Pieces Together) [54]

Rnd 33: ch 1, (sc 7, sc2tog) 6 times, join with sl st in first st [48]

Rnds 34-35: sc in each st around [48]

Rnd 36: sl st in each st around [48]

Invisible fasten off and weave in all ends.

Add stitches for the mouth and cheeks using **black** and **red** yarn (see Making Up: Stitching Facial Details).

Begin shaping by inserting needle from the center bottom to the center top, insert the needle back down from the center top to slightly off the center bottom. Insert the needle from the center bottom to the center top. Pull to create an indentation in the bottom of the cup. Finish off and weave in the ends.

JUICE

Rnd 1: with **orange** yarn, sc 6 in magic loop [6]

Rnd 2: 2 sc in each st around [12]

Rnd 3: (sc 1, 2 sc in next st) 6 times [18]

Rnd 4: (sc 2, 2 sc in next st) 6 times [24]

Rnd 5: (sc 3, 2 sc in next st) 6 times [30]

Rnd 6: (sc 4, 2 sc in next st) 6 times [36]

Rnd 7: (sc 5, 2 sc in next st) 6 times [42]

Rnd 8: (sc 6, 2 sc in next st) 6 times [48]

Rnd 9: (sc 7, 2 sc in next st) 6 times [54]

Invisible fasten off and weave in the ends.

ORANGE SLICE (MAKE 2)

Rnd 1: with **white** yarn, sc 6 in magic loop [6]

Rnd 2: change to **orange** yarn, 2 sc in each st around [12]

You will now be turning your work at the end of each row to create a "cut" in the orange slice to fit over the cup.

Row 3: ch 1, (sc 1, 2 sc in next st) 6 times, turn [18]

Row 4: ch 1, (sc 2, 2 sc in next st) 6 times, turn [24]

Row 5: change to **white** yarn, ch 1, (sc 3, 2 sc in next st) 6 times, turn [30]

Row 6: change to **orange** yarn, ch 1, sc in each st around [30]

Invisible fasten off and weave in the ends. With **white** yarn and a yarn needle, stitch on 6 segment lines. Make a second **orange** slice, but do not cut your yarn after row 6.

With the right sides facing out, place the second orange slice on top of the first slice. With the **orange** yarn used to make the second slice, sl st around both orange slices to join them together. Attach the orange slice to the edge of the cup.

PUMPKIN

Materials

- 3.25mm (D/3) crochet hook

- Paintbox Yarns Cotton Aran yarn: one 50g (1.75oz) ball each of Blood Orange (**orange**) and Grass Green (**green**)
- 8mm safety eyes
- Scraps of **yellow** and **black** yarn
- Fiberfill stuffing
- Yarn needle
- Stitch marker

Finished Size

10cm (4in) tall by 11.5cm (4^1/$_2$in) wide

Gauge

5 sc sts and 6 rows = 2.5cm (1in)

PUMPKIN

Beginning at the bottom of the pumpkin:

Rnd 1: with **orange** yarn working in BLO, sc 7 in magic loop [7]

Rnd 2: working in BLO, 2 sc in each st around [14]

Rnd 3: working in BLO, (sc 1, 2 sc in next st) 7 times [21]

Rnd 4: working in BLO, (sc 2, 2 sc in next st) 7 times [28]

Rnd 5: working in BLO, (sc 3, 2 sc in next st) 7 times [35]

Rnd 6: working in BLO, (sc 4, 2 sc in next st) 7 times [42]

Rnd 7: working in BLO, (sc 5, 2 sc in next st) 7 times [49]

Rnd 8: working in BLO, (sc 6, 2 sc in next st) 7 times [56]

Rnd 9: working in BLO, (sc 7, 2 sc in next st) 7 times [63]

Rnds 10-19: working in BLO, sc in each st around [63]

Rnd 20: working in BLO, (sc 7, sc2tog) 7 times [56]

Rnd 21: working in BLO, (sc 3, sc2tog, sc 3) 7 times [49]

Rnd 22: working in BLO, (sc 5, sc2tog) 7 times [42]

Place 8mm safety eyes between **Rnds 15 and 16** with 5 sts in between. Begin to stuff with fiberfill.

Rnd 23: working in BLO, (sc 2, sc2tog, sc 2) 7 times [35]

Rnd 24: working in BLO, (sc 3, sc2tog) 7 times [28]

Rnd 25: working in BLO, (sc 1, sc2tog, sc 1) 7 times [21]

Rnd 26: working in BLO, (sc 1, sc2tog) 7 times [14]

Rnd 27: working in BLO, (sc2tog) 7 times [6]

Finish stuffing. Fasten off and leave a long 102cm (40in) yarn tail.

With the yarn needle, weave the yarn through BLO to close the opening and insert the needle from the center top to the center bottom.

To make the indented ridges in the pumpkin, start at the center bottom. Insert the needle under the front loops moving toward the top center (1).

Insert the needle from center top to the center bottom (2). Pull the yarn to create an indented ridge in the pumpkin.

2

Repeat the above steps until you have 7 indented ridges in total. Each ridge is 8 stitches apart when counting on **Rnd 15** and the very first ridge is made in the center between the eyes (3 and 4).

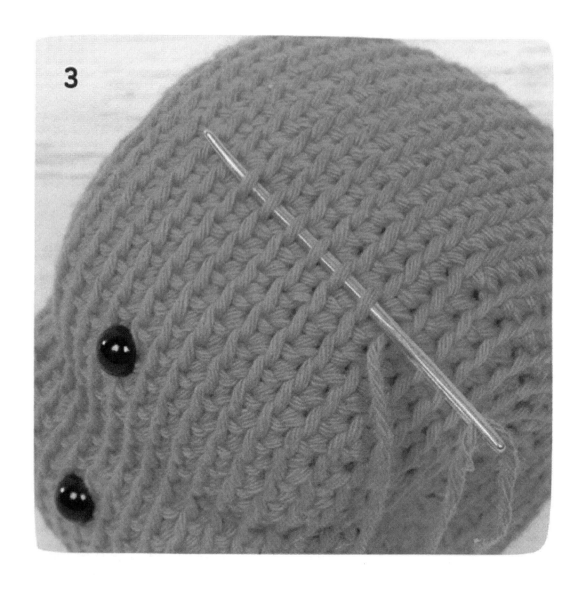

When finished secure the yarn with two or three knots and weave in the end.

Add stitches for the mouth and cheeks using **black** and **yellow** yarn (see Making Up: Stitching Facial Details).

STEM

Rnd 1: with **green** yarn, sc 6 in magic loop [6]

Rnds 2-7: sc in each st around [6]

Rnd 8: 2 sc in each st around [12]

Rnd 9: (sc 2, 2 sc in next st) 4 times [16]

Rnd 10: (sc 3, 2 sc in next st) 4 times [20]

Do not stuff. Fasten off and leave a long yarn tail.

Sew the stem onto the pumpkin by sewing into the stitches from **Rnd 10** of the stem and into the front loops from **Rnd 25** of the pumpkin (see Making Up: Sewing Two Pieces Together). Finish off and weave in all ends.

Yellow is the color of happiness! Yellow is the brightest and most visible color on the spectrum. Words often associated with this color are sunshine, happiness, humor, creativity, and fun. The color yellow can help with decision making as it relates to clarity of thoughts and ideas.

BANANA

Materials

- 3.25mm (D/3) crochet hook
- Paintbox Yarns Cotton Aran yarn: one 50g (1.75oz) ball each of Paper White (**white**), Daffodil Yellow (**yellow**), and Coffee Bean (**brown**)
- 6mm safety eyes
- Scraps of **pink** and **black** yarn
- Fiberfill stuffing
- Yarn needle
- Stitch marker

Finished Size

12.5cm (5in) tall by 5cm (2in) wide

Gauge

5 sc sts and 6 rows = 2.5cm (1in)

BANANA

Rnd 1: with **white** yarn, sc 6 in magic loop [6]

Rnd 2: 2 sc in each st around [12]

Rnd 3: sc in each st around [12]

Rnd 4: (sc 2, 2 sc in next st) 4 times [16]

Rnds 5-12: sc in each st around [16]

Rnd 13: (sc 7, 2 sc in next st) twice [18]

Rnd 14: change to **yellow** yarn, working in FLO, (sc 3, ch 10, sc in 2nd ch from hook, 1 sc in next 8 ch sts, sc 3) 3 times

Rnd 15: (sl st, skip next 2 sts, dc 6, hdc 2, sc 1, sc + ch 3 + sl st in skipped ch st from rnd 14, sc 1, hdc 2, dc 6, skip next 2 sts, sl st 1) 3 times

Place 6mm safety eyes between **Rnds 6 and 7** with 2 sts in between and positioned so that they are centered between two sections of peel. Begin to stuff with fiberfill.

Rnd 16: working in BLO from **Rnd 14**, sc in each st around [18]

Rnds 17-25: sc in each st around [18]

Rnd 26: (sc 1, sc2tog) 6 times [12]

Rnd 27: sc in each st around [12]

Rnd 28: (sc2tog) 6 times [6]

Rnd 29: change to **brown** yarn, sc in each st around [6]

Finish stuffing. Fasten off and leave a long yarn tail. With a yarn needle, weave the tail through FLO to close the opening. Weave in the ends.

Add stitches for the mouth and cheeks using **black** and **pink** yarn (see Making Up: Stitching Facial Details).

Banana Peel Chart

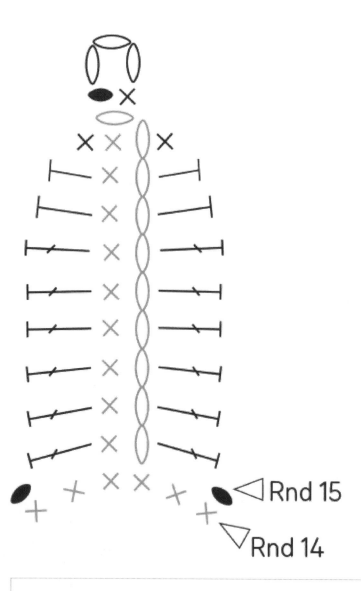

Rnd 15

Rnd 14

NOT PEELING WELL?

Make and give one as a gift to someone who's not feeling well.
Just add a tag that says, "I hope you peel better!"

LEMON

Materials

- 3.25mm (D/3) crochet hook
- Paintbox Yarns Cotton Aran yarn: one 50g (1.75oz) ball each of Daffodil Yellow (**yellow**) and Lime Green (**green**)
- 7mm safety eyes
- Scraps of **green** and **black** yarn
- Fiberfill stuffing
- Yarn needle
- Stitch marker

Finished Size

10cm (4in) tall by 6cm (2^1/$_2$in) wide

Gauge

5 sc sts and 6 rows = 2.5cm (1in)

LEMON

Beginning at the bottom of the lemon:

Rnd 1: with **yellow** yarn, sc 6 in magic loop [6]

Rnd 2: 2 sc in each st around [12]

Rnd 3: sc in each st around [12]

Rnd 4: (sc 1, 2 sc in next st) 6 times [18]

Rnd 5: (sc 2, 2 sc in next st) 6 times [24]

Rnd 6: (sc 3, 2 sc in next st) 6 times [30]

Rnd 7: (sc 4, 2 sc in next st) 6 times [36]

Rnds 8-16: sc in each st around [36]

Place 7mm safety eyes between **Rnds 10 and 11** with 3 sts in between. Begin to stuff with fiberfill.

Rnd 17: (sc 4, sc2tog) 6 times [30]

Rnd 18: (sc 3, sc2tog) 6 times [24]

Rnd 19: (sc 2, sc2tog) 6 times [18]

Rnd 20: sc in each st around [18]

Rnd 21: (sc 1, sc2tog) 6 times [12]

Rnds 22-23: sc in each st around [12]

Rnd 24: (sc2tog) 6 times [6]

Finish stuffing. Fasten off and leave a long yarn tail. With a yarn needle, weave the tail through FLO to close the opening. Weave in all ends.

Add stitches for the mouth and cheeks using **black** and **green** yarn (see Making Up: Stitching Facial Details).

LEAF

With **green** yarn, ch 10.

Rnd 1: sl st in 2nd ch from hook, sc 1, hdc 1, dc 4, hdc 1, sc 3 in last st, working on the other side of the foundation ch, hdc 1, dc 4, hdc 1, sc 1, sl st 1, sl st in beginning skipped ch st.

Invisible fasten off (see Finishing: Invisible Fasten Off) and weave in all ends. Attach to the top front of the lemon.

Leaf Chart

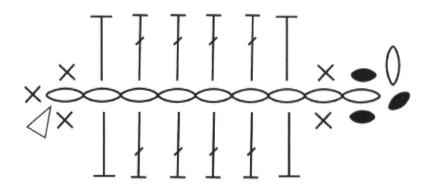

SCHOOL PENCIL

Materials

- 3.25mm (D/3) crochet hook
- Paintbox Yarns Cotton Aran yarn: one 50g (1.75oz) ball each of Bubblegum Pink (**pink**), Stormy Grey (**gray**), Buttercup Yellow (**yellow**), Light Caramel (**tan**), and Pure Black (**black**)
- 6mm safety eyes
- Scrap of **black** yarn
- Fiberfill stuffing
- Yarn needle
- Stitch marker

Finished Size

9cm (3$\frac{1}{2}$in) tall by 4cm (1$\frac{1}{2}$in) wide

Gauge

5 sc sts and 6 rows = 2.5cm (1in)

PENCIL

Rnd 1: with **pink** yarn, sc 6 in magic loop [6]

Rnd 2: 2 sc in each st around [12]

Rnd 3: (sc 3, 2 sc in next st) 3 times [15]

Rnd 4: working in BLO, sc in each st around [15]

Rnds 5-6: sc in each st around [15]

Rnd 7: change to **gray** yarn, sc in each st around [15]

Rnd 8: working in BLO, sc in each st around [15]

Rnd 9: change to **yellow** yarn, working in BLO, sc in each st around [15]

Rnds 10-16: sc in each st around [15]

Place 6mm safety eyes between **Rnds 13 and 14** with 2 sts in between. Begin to stuff with fiberfill.

Rnd 17: change to **tan** yarn, (sc2tog, sc 3) 3 times [12]

Rnd 18: sc in each st around [12]

Rnd 19: (sc2tog, sc 2) 3 times [9]

Rnd 20: change to **black** yarn, (sc2tog, sc 1) 3 times [6]

Finish stuffing. Fasten off and leave a long yarn tail. With a yarn needle, weave the tail through FLO to close the opening. Weave in all ends.

Add stitches for the mouth using **black** yarn (see Making Up: Stitching Facial Details).

LEMON CAKE

Materials

- 2.75mm (C/2) and 3.25mm (D/3) crochet hooks
- Paintbox Yarns Cotton Aran yarn: one 50g (1.75oz) ball each of Paper White (**white**), Daffodil Yellow (**light yellow**) and Buttercup Yellow (**dark yellow**)
- Paintbox Yarns Cotton DK yarn: one 50g (1.75oz) ball each of Paper White (**white**), Daffodil Yellow (**light yellow**), Buttercup Yellow (**dark yellow**) and Lime Green (**green**)
- 7mm safety eyes
- Scraps of **green** and **black** yarn
- Fiberfill stuffing
- Yarn needle
- Stitch marker

Finished Size

10cm (4in) tall by 7.5cm (3in) wide

Gauge

5 sc sts and 6 rows = 2.5cm (1in) using Aran yarn

6 sc sts and 7 rows = 2.5cm (1in) using DK yarn

CAKE

Use Aran weight yarn throughout for the cake and the frosting.

Beginning at the top of the cake:

Rnd 1: with **3.25mm** hook and **white** yarn, sc 6 in magic loop [6]

Rnd 2: 2 sc in each st around [12]

Rnd 3: (sc 1, 2 sc in next st) 6 times [18]

Rnd 4: (sc 2, 2 sc in next st) 6 times [24]

Rnd 5: (sc 3, 2 sc in next st) 6 times [30]

Rnd 6: (sc 4, 2 sc in next st) 6 times [36]

Rnd 7: (sc 5, 2 sc in next st) 6 times [42]

Rnd 8: working in BLO, sc in each st around [42]

Rnd 9: change to **light yellow** yarn, sc in each st around [42]

Rnds 10-11: sc in each st around [42]

Rnd 12: change to **white** yarn, sc in each st around [42]

Rnd 13: change to **dark yellow** yarn, sc in each st around [42]

Rnd 14: change to **light yellow** yarn, sc in each st around [42]

Rnds 15-16: sc in each st around [42]

Rnd 17: change to **white** yarn, sc in each st around [42]

Rnd 18: change to **dark yellow** yarn, sc in each st around [42]

Rnd 19: change to **light yellow** yarn, sc in each st around [42]

Rnds 20-21: sc in each st around [42]

Place 7mm safety eyes between **Rnds 13 and 14** with 4 sts in between. Begin to stuff with fiberfill.

Rnd 22: working in BLO, (sc 5, sc2tog) 6 times [36]

Rnd 23: (sc 4, sc2tog) 6 times [30]

Rnd 24: (sc 3, sc2tog) 6 times [24]

Rnd 25: (sc 2, sc2tog) 6 times [18]

Rnd 26: (sc 1, sc2tog) 6 times [12]

Rnd 27: (sc2tog) 6 times [6]

Finish stuffing. Fasten off and leave a long yarn tail. With a yarn needle, weave the tail through FLO to close the opening.

Begin shaping by inserting the needle from the center bottom to the center top. Insert the needle back down from the center top to slightly off the center bottom. Insert the needle from the center bottom to the center top. Pull to create an indentation in the bottom of the cake. Finish off and weave in all ends.

With the **white** edge of the cake at the top, add stitches for the mouth and cheeks using **black** and **green** yarn (see Making Up: Stitching Facial Details).

FROSTING

Row 1: with **3.25mm** hook and **white** yarn (ch 4, 5-dc-bl (see Special Stitches: 5-Double Crochet Bobble) in 4th ch from hook) 12 times, ch 1 [12 bobble sts]

Fasten off and weave in all ends. Attach to the top edge of the cake.

LEMON (MAKE 3)

Use DK weight yarn throughout for the lemons.

Rnd 1: with **2.75mm** hook and **white** yarn, sc 6 in magic loop [6]

Rnd 2: change to **light yellow** yarn, 2 sc in each st around [12]

Rnd 3: (sc 1, 2 sc in next st) 6 times [18]

Rnd 4: (sc 2, 2 sc in next st) 6 times [24]

Rnd 5: change to **white** yarn, (sc 3, 2 sc in next st) 6 times [30]

Rnd 6: change to **dark yellow** yarn, sc in each st around [30]

Do not cut the yarn. With **white** yarn and the yarn needle stitch 6 segment lines as shown (1).

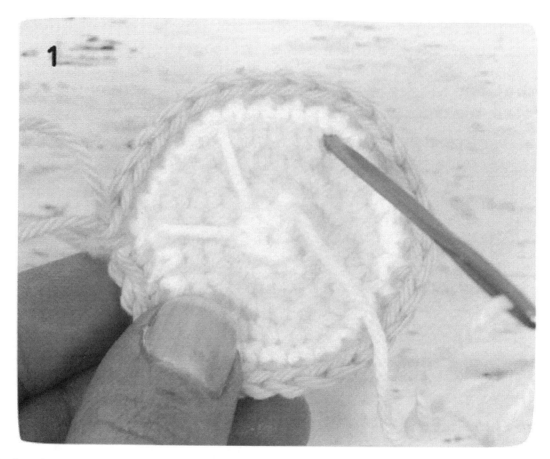

Fold the lemon in half (2).

With the same yarn used to crochet **Rnd 6**, sl st in both stitches of **Rnd 6** of the lemon to join the two sides together (3).

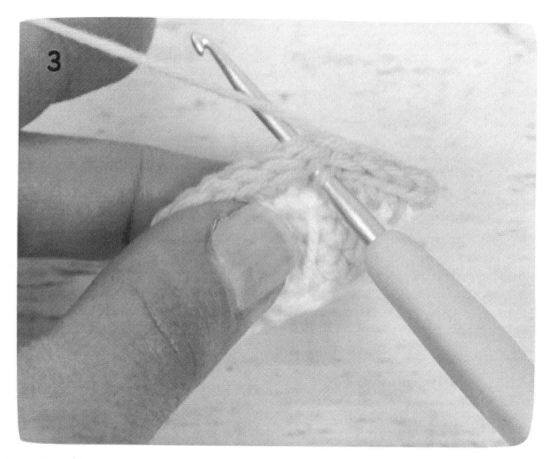

Finish off and weave in all ends. Attach two lemons to the top of the cake and one to the side of the cake.

WHIPPED CREAM

Use Aran weight yarn for the whipped cream.

With **3.25mm** hook and **white** yarn, ch 36.

Row 1: hdc in 2nd ch from hook, hdc 34 [35]

Fasten off and leave a long yarn tail. With the yarn needle use the tail to sew the whipped cream into a spiral. Attach to the top of the cake.

LEAF (MAKE 2)

With **2.75mm** hook and **green** yarn, ch 7.

Row 1: sl st in 2nd ch from hook, sc 1, hdc 1, dc 1, hdc 1, sc 3 in last st, working on the other side of the foundation ch, hdc 1, dc 1, hdc 1, sc 1, sl st in beginning skipped ch st [13]

Invisible fasten off (see Finishing: Invisible Fasten Off) and weave in all ends. Attach to the top of the cake.

MUSTARD BOTTLE

Materials

- 2.75mm (C/2) crochet hook
- Paintbox Yarns Cotton DK yarn: one 50g (1.75oz) ball of Buttercup Yellow (**yellow**)
- 6mm safety eyes
- Scraps of **orange** and **black** yarn
- Fiberfill stuffing
- Yarn needle
- Stitch marker

Finished Size

13cm (5in) tall by 5cm (2in) wide

Gauge

6 sc sts and 7 rows = 2.5cm (1in)

BOTTLE

Rnd 1: with **yellow** yarn, sc 4 in magic loop [4]

Rnd 2: sc in each st around [4]

Rnd 3: (sc 1, 2 sc in next st) twice [6]

Rnd 4: sc in each st around [6]

Rnd 5: (sc 2, 2 sc in next st) twice [8]

Rnd 6: sc in each st around [8]

Rnd 7: (sc 3, 2 sc in next st) twice [10]

Rnd 8: sc in each st around [10]

Rnd 9: working in FLO, 2 sc in each st around [20]

Rnd 10: (sc 1, 2 sc in next st) 10 times [30]

Rnd 11: working in BLO, sc in each st around [30]

Rnd 12: sc in each st around [30]

Rnd 13: working in FLO, (sc 2, 2 sc in next st) 10 times [40]

Rnd 14: working in BLO, sc in each st around [40]

Rnd 15: (sc 8, sc2tog) 4 times [36]

Rnds 16-37: sc in each st around [36]

Place 6mm safety eyes between **Rnds 28 and 29** with 4 sts in between. Begin to stuff with fiberfill.

Rnd 38: working in BLO, (sc 4, sc2tog) 6 times [30]

Rnd 39: (sc 3, sc2tog) 6 times [24]

Rnd 40: (sc 2, sc2tog) 6 times [18]

Rnd 41: (sc 1, sc2tog) 6 times [12]

Rnd 42: (sc2tog) 6 times [6]

Finish stuffing. Fasten off and leave a long yarn tail. With a yarn needle, weave the tail through FLO to close the opening.

Begin shaping by inserting the needle from the center bottom to the center top. Insert the needle back down from the center top to slightly off the center bottom. Insert the needle from the center bottom to the center top. Pull to create an indentation in the bottom of the bottle. Finish off and weave in all ends.

Add stitches for the mouth and cheeks using **black** and **orange** yarn (see Making Up: Stitching Facial Details).

I MUSTARD-MIT...

Not a fan of mustard? Then make a ketchup bottle instead; simply exchange the yellow yarn for red. Or make a complete pair—it would be quite saucy!

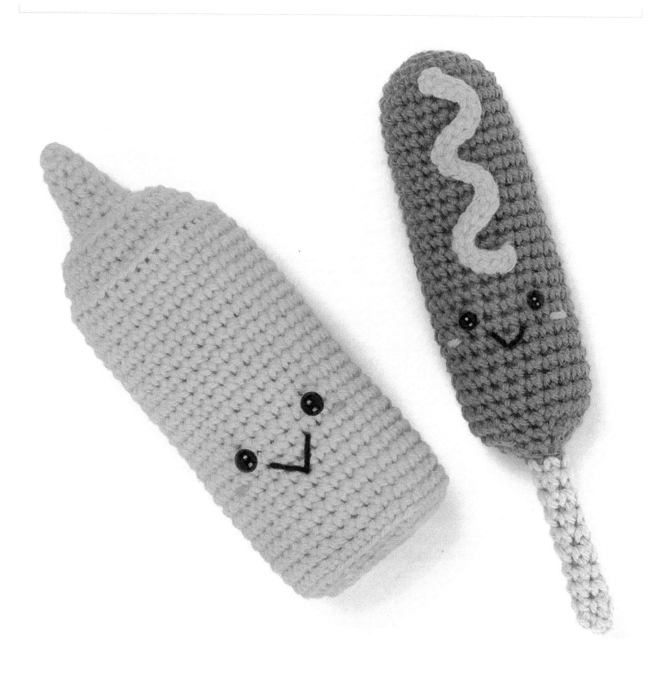

GREEN

Green is the color of nature.
It symbolizes life, growth,
and rebirth. It can help us
feel balanced, calm, fresh,
and reinvigorated. Green is
the color of goodness for the
earth and for health.

BRUSSEL SPROUT

Materials

- 3.25mm (D/3) crochet hook
- Paintbox Yarns Cotton Aran yarn: one 50g (1.75oz) ball of Grass Green (**green**)
- 7mm safety eyes
- Scraps of **pink** and **black** yarn
- Fiberfill stuffing
- T-pins
- Yarn needle
- Stitch marker

Finished Size

6.5cm (2$\frac{1}{2}$in) tall by 6.5cm (2$\frac{1}{2}$in) wide

Gauge

5 sc sts and 6 rows = 2.5cm (1in)

BRUSSEL SPROUT

Rnd 1: with **green** yarn, sc 6 in magic loop [6]

Rnd 2: 2 sc in each st around [12]

Rnd 3: (sc 1, 2 sc in next st) 6 times [18]

Rnd 4: (sc 2, 2 sc in next st) 6 times [24]

Rnd 5: (sc 3, 2 sc in next st) 6 times [30]

Rnds 6-10: sc in each st around [30]

Place 7mm safety eyes between **Rnds 4 and 5** with 3 sts in between. Begin to stuff with fiberfill.

Rnd 11: (sc 3, sc2tog) 6 times [24]

Rnd 12: (sc 2, sc2tog) 6 times [18]

Rnd 13: (sc 1, sc2tog) 6 times [12]

Rnd 14: (sc2tog) 6 times [6]

Finish stuffing. Fasten off and leave a long yarn tail. With a yarn needle, weave the tail through FLO to close the opening. Weave in all ends.

Add stitches for the mouth and cheeks using **black** and **pink** yarn (see Making Up: Stitching Facial Details).

LEAF (MAKE 3)

Rnd 1: with **green** yarn, sc 6 in magic loop [6]

Rnd 2: 2 sc in each st around [12]

Rnd 3: (sc 1, 2 sc in next st) 6 times [18]

Rnd 4: (sc 2, 2 sc in next st) 6 times [24]

Rnd 5: (sc 3, 2 sc in next st) 6 times [30]

Rnd 6: sc in each st around [30]

Invisible fasten off (see Finishing: Invisible Fasten Off) and weave in all ends.

Pin the leaves into place and then attach to the brussel sprout, leaving the tops of the leaves unattached so they can be folded down (1-3).

1

2

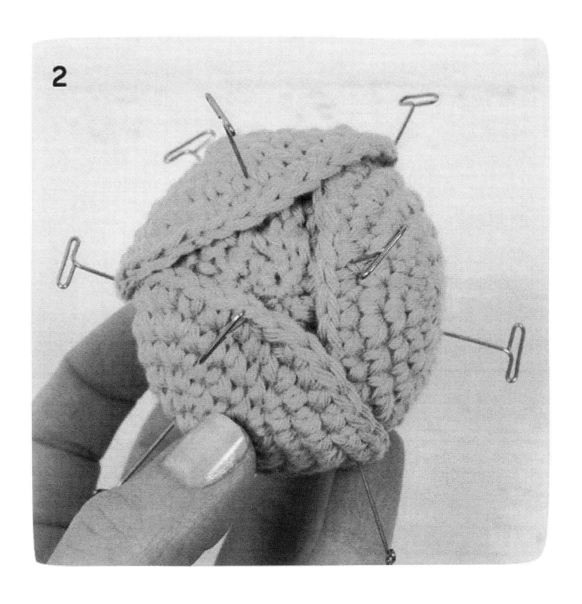

3

EVERYDAY I'M BRUSSELIN'...

Make a whole bowl full of sprouts for a cute centerpiece at Christmas.

CHRISTMAS TREE

Materials

- 2.75mm (C/2) and 3.25mm (D/3) crochet hooks
- Paintbox Yarns Cotton Aran yarn: one 50g (1.75oz) ball each of Grass Green (**green**) and Coffee Bean (**brown**)
- Paintbox Yarns Cotton DK yarn: one 50g (1.75oz) ball of Buttercup Yellow (**yellow**)
- 7mm safety eyes
- Scraps of **light green** and **black** yarn
- Fiberfill stuffing
- Yarn needle
- Stitch marker

Finished Size

13cm (5in) tall by 6.5cm (2$\frac{1}{2}$in) wide

Gauge

5 sc sts and 6 rows = 2.5cm (1in) using Aran yarn

TREE

Rnd 1: with **3.25mm** hook and **brown** yarn, sc 6 in magic loop [6]

Rnd 2: 2 sc in each st around [12]

Rnd 3: working in BLO, sc in each st around [12]

Rnds 4-7: sc in each st around [12]

Rnd 8: change to **green** yarn, working in FLO, (sc 1, 2 sc in next st) 6 times [18]

Rnd 9: (sc 2, 2 sc in next st) 6 times [24]

Rnd 10: (sc 3, 2 sc in next st) 6 times [30]

Rnd 11: working in BLO, sc in each st around [30]

Rnds 12-13: sc in each st around [30]

Rnd 14: (sc 3, sc2tog) 6 times [24]

Rnds 15-16: sc in each st around [24]

Rnd 17: working in BLO, sc in each st around [24]

Place 7mm safety eyes between **Rnds 13 and 14** with 4 sts in between. Begin to stuff with fiberfill.

Rnd 18: (sc 2, sc2tog) 6 times [18]

Rnd 19: sc in each st around [18]

Rnd 20: working in BLO, sc in each st around [18]

Rnd 21: sc in each st around [18]

Rnd 22: (sc 1, sc2tog) 6 times [12]

Rnd 23: working in BLO, sc in each st around [12]

Rnds 24-25: sc in each st around [12]

Rnd 26: (sc2tog) 6 times [6]

Finish stuffing. Fasten off and leave a long yarn tail. With a yarn needle, weave the tail through FLO to close the opening. Weave in all ends.

Add stitches for the mouth and cheeks using **black** and **light green** yarn (see Making Up: Stitching Facial Details).

With the top of the tree pointing down, join **green** yarn in any front loop from **Rnd 11**, working in FLO, (ch 2, sc 1) to end of rnd. Repeat the same in the front loops from **Rnds 17, 20 and 23.**

STAR

Rnd 1: with **2.75mm** hook and **yellow** yarn, sc 5 in magic loop [5]

Rnd 2: (ch 3, sl st in 2nd ch from hook, sc in next ch, sl st in next st from rnd 1) 5 times

Invisible fasten off (see Finishing: Invisible Fasten Off) and weave in all ends. Attach the star to the top of the tree.

HO HO HO...

Use DK yarn to make a string of fairy lights (see Christmas Light in Red section), in all the colors of the rainbow. Use 5mm safety eyes, and make a chain with green yarn by working ch 10, sl st in 10th ch from hook, repeat (ch 20, sl st in the top of a light) until you have joined all your lights, ch 30, sl st in the tenth ch from hook. Fasten off and weave in the ends. Tie a knot where both slip stitches were made at the beginning and end of the lights.

ST PATRICK'S DAY CAKE

Materials

- 2.75mm (C/2) and 3.25mm (D/3) crochet hooks
- Paintbox Yarns Cotton Aran yarn: one 50g (1.75oz) ball each of Grass Green (**green**), Paper White (**white**), Racing Green (**dark green**), and Pure Black (**black**).
- Paintbox Yarns Cotton DK yarn: one 50g (1.75oz) ball each of Lime Green (**lime**) and Daffodil Yellow (**yellow**)
- 7mm safety eyes
- Scraps of **pink** and **black** yarn
- Fiberfill stuffing
- Yarn needle
- Stitch marker

Finished Size

13cm (5in) tall by 7.5cm (3in) wide

Gauge

5 sc sts and 6 rows = 2.5cm (1in) using Aran yarn

CAKE

Rnd 1: with **3.25mm** hook and **green** yarn, sc 6 in magic loop [6]
Rnd 2: 2 sc in each st around [12]

Rnd 3: (sc 1, 2 sc in next st) 6 times [18]

Rnd 4: (sc 2, 2 sc in next st) 6 times [24]

Rnd 5: (sc 3, 2 sc in next st) 6 times [30]

Rnd 6: (sc 4, 2 sc in next st) 6 times [36]

Rnd 7: (sc 5, 2 sc in next st) 6 times [42]

Rnd 8: working in BLO, sc in each st around [42]

Rnds 9-10: sc in each st around [42]

Rnd 11: change to **white** yarn, sc in each st around [42]

Rnd 12: change to **green** yarn, sc in each st around [42]

Rnds 13-14: sc in each st around [42]

Rnd 15: change to **white** yarn, sc in each st around [42]

Rnd 16: change to **green** yarn, sc in each st around [42]

Rnds 17-18: sc in each st around [42]

Place 7mm safety eyes between **Rnds 12 and 13** with 4 sts in between. Begin to stuff with fiberfill.

Rnd 19: working in BLO, (sc 5, sc2tog) 6 times [36]

Rnd 20: (sc 4, sc2tog) 6 times [30]

Rnd 21: (sc 3, sc2tog) 6 times [24]

Rnd 22: (sc 2, sc2tog) 6 times [18]

Rnd 23: (sc 1, sc2tog) 6 times [12]

Rnd 24: (sc2tog) 6 times [6]

Finish stuffing. Fasten off and leave a long yarn tail. With a yarn needle weave the tail through FLO to close opening.

Add stitches for the mouth and cheeks using **black** and **pink** yarn (see Making Up: Stitching Facial Details).

Begin shaping by inserting the needle from the center bottom to the center top, insert the needle back down from the center top to slightly off the center bottom. Insert the needle from the center bottom to the center top. Pull to create an indentation in the bottom of the cake. Finish off and weave in all ends.

GREEN FROSTING

Row 1: with **3.25mm** hook and **green** yarn (ch 4, 5-dc-bl (see Special Stitches: 5-Double Crochet Bobble) in 4th ch from hook) 12 times, ch 1 [12 bobble sts]

Fasten off and weave in the ends. Attach to the bottom edge of the cake.

WHITE FROSTING

Rnd 1: with **3.25mm** hook and **white** yarn, sc 6 in magic loop [6]

Rnd 2: 2 sc in each st around [12]

Rnd 3: (sc 1, 2 sc in next st) 6 times [18]

Rnd 4: (sc 2, 2 sc in next st) 6 times [24]

Rnd 5: (sc 3, 2 sc in next st) 6 times [30]

Rnd 6: (sc 4, 2 sc in next st) 6 times [36]

Rnd 7: (sc 5, 2 sc in next st) 6 times [42]

Rnd 8: (sc 6, 2 sc in next st) 6 times [48]

Rnd 9: working in BLO, (sc 1, hdc 1, dc 1, tr 1, dc 1, hdc 1, sc 2, hdc 1, dc 1, tr 1, 2 tr in next st, tr 1, dc 1, hdc 1, sc 1) 3 times [51]

Invisible fasten off (see Finishing: Invisible Fasten Off) and weave in all ends. Attach to the top of the cake.

LEPRECHAUN HAT

Rnd 1: with **3.25mm** hook and **dark green** yarn, sc 6 in magic loop [6]

Rnd 2: 2 sc in each st around [12]

Rnd 3: (sc 1, 2 sc in next st) 6 times [18]

Rnd 4: (sc 2, 2 sc in next st) 6 times [24]

Rnd 5: (sc 3, 2 sc in next st) 6 times [30]

Rnd 6: working in BLO, sc in each st around [30]

Rnd 7: (sc 3, sc2tog) 6 times [24]

Rnds 8-10: sc in each st around [24]

Rnd 11: change to **black** yarn, sc in each st around [24]

Rnds 12-13: sc in each st around [24]

Rnd 14: change to **dark green** yarn, working in FLO, (2 sc in next st, sc 2) 8 times [32]

Rnd 15: (2 sc in next st, sc 3) 8 times [40]

Rnd 16: (2 sc in next st, sc 4) 8 times [48]

Invisible fasten off (see Finishing: Invisible Fasten Off) and weave in all ends. Stuff the hat with fiberfill and attach it to the top of the cake.

BUCKLE

With **2.75mm** hook and **yellow** yarn, ch 6, sl st in first ch to make a circle.

Rnd 1: (3 sc, ch 1) 4 times into the circle, join with sl st in the first st.

Fasten off and weave in the ends. Attach to the front of the hat.

FOUR-LEAF CLOVER

With **2.75mm** hook and **lime** yarn, ch 4, sl st in first ch to make a circle.

Rnd 1: (ch 3, dc 1, hdc 1, dc 1, ch 3, sl st 1) 4 times into the circle, ch 6, hdc in 3rd ch from hook, sl st in next 3 ch, sl st into the center of the circle.

Fasten off and weave in the ends. Attach to the front of the hat next to the buckle.

PEAR

Materials

- 3.25mm (D/3) crochet hook
- Paintbox Yarns Cotton Aran yarn: one 50g (1.75oz) ball each of Lime Green (**lime**), Grass Green (**green**), and Coffee Bean (**brown**)
- 8mm safety eyes
- Scraps of **light green** and **black** yarn
- Fiberfill stuffing
- Yarn needle
- Stitch marker

Finished Size

14cm ($5^1/_2$in) tall by 9cm ($3^1/_2$in) wide

Gauge

5 sc sts and 6 rows = 2.5cm (1in)

PEAR

Rnd 1: with **lime** yarn, sc 6 in magic loop [6]

Rnd 2: 2 sc in each st around [12]

Rnd 3: (sc 1, 2 sc in next st) 6 times [18]

Rnds 4-5: sc in each st around [18]

Rnd 6: (sc 2, 2 sc in next st) 6 times [24]

Rnds 7-10: sc in each st around [24]

Rnd 11: (sc 3, 2 sc in next st) 6 times [30]

Rnds 12-16: sc in each st around [30]

Rnd 17: (sc 4, 2 sc in next st) 6 times [36]

Rnd 18: (sc 5, 2 sc in next st) 6 times [42]

Rnd 19: (sc 6, 2 sc in next st) 6 times [48]

Rnd 20: (sc 7, 2 sc in next st) 6 times [54]

Rnds 21-26: sc in each st around [54]

Rnd 27: (sc2tog, sc 7) 6 times [48]

Rnd 28: (sc 3, sc2tog, sc 3) 6 times [42]

Rnd 29: (sc2tog, sc 5) 6 times [36]

Place 8mm safety eyes between **Rnds 20 and 21** with 5 sts in between. Begin to stuff with fiberfill.

Rnd 30: (sc 2, sc2tog, sc 2) 6 times [30]

Rnd 31: (sc2tog, sc 3) 6 times [24]

Rnd 32: (sc 1, sc2tog, sc 1) 6 times [18]

Rnd 33: (sc2tog, sc 1) 6 times [12]

Rnd 34: (sc2tog) 6 times [6]

Finish stuffing. Fasten off and leave a long yarn tail. With a yarn needle weave the tail through FLO to close opening.

Begin shaping by inserting the needle from the center bottom to the center top, insert needle back down from slightly off the center top to slightly off the center bottom. Pull the yarn to create a slight indentation in the top of the pear.

Insert the needle from the center bottom to the center top. Pull to create an indentation in the bottom of the pear. Finish off and weave in all ends.

Add stitches for the mouth and cheeks using **black** and **light green** yarn (see Making Up: Stitching Facial Details).

LEAF

With **green** yarn, ch 10.

Rnd 1: sl st in 2nd ch from hook, sc 1, hdc 1, dc 4, hdc 1, sc 3 in last st, working on the other side of the foundation ch, hdc 1, dc 4, hdc 1, sc 1, sl st 1, sl st in beginning skipped ch st.

Invisible fasten off (see Finishing: Invisible Fasten Off) and weave in all ends. Attach to the top of the pear.

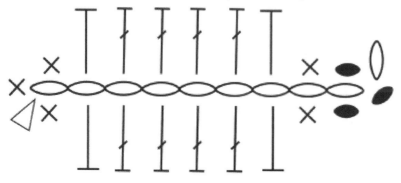

STEM

With 2 strands of **brown** yarn, ch 9.

Row 1: working in back bump loops (see Special Stitches: Back Bump), sc in 2nd ch from hook, sl st 7.

Fasten off and weave in all ends. Attach to the top of the pear.

Leaf Chart

STRIVE FOR PEAR-FECTION...

Marking your rounds with a stitch marker ensures that your amigurumi turns out perfectly. Don't have a stitch marker? A safety pin, paper clip, bobby pin, or contrasting color of yarn works just as well.

PEAS IN A POD

Materials

- 3.25mm (D/3) crochet hook
- Paintbox Yarns Cotton Aran yarn: one 50g (1.75oz) ball each of Lime Green (**lime**) and Grass Green (**green**)
- 7mm safety eyes
- Scraps of **pink** and **black** yarn
- Fiberfill stuffing
- Yarn needle
- Stitch marker

Finished Size

5.5cm (2$\frac{1}{4}$in) tall by 15cm (6in) wide

Gauge

5 sc sts and 6 rows = 2.5cm (1in)

PEAS (MAKE 3)

Rnd 1: with **lime** yarn, sc 6 in magic loop [6]

Rnd 2: 2 sc in each st around [12]

Rnd 3: (sc 1, 2 sc in next st) 6 times [18]

Rnd 4: (sc 2, 2 sc in next st) 6 times [24]

Rnd 5: (sc 3, 2 sc in next st) 6 times [30]

Rnds 6-10: sc in each st around [30]

Place 6mm safety eyes between **Rnds 6 and 7** with 3 sts in between. Begin to stuff with fiberfill.

Rnd 11: (sc 3, sc2tog) 6 times [24]

Rnd 12: (sc 2, sc2tog) 6 times [18]

Rnd 13: (sc 1, sc2tog) 6 times [12]

Rnd 14: (sc2tog) 6 times [6]

Finish stuffing. Fasten off and leave a long yarn tail. With a yarn needle weave the tail through FLO to close opening. Weave in all ends.

Add stitches for the mouth and cheeks using **black** and **pink** yarn (see Making Up: Stitching Facial Details).

POD

With **green** yarn, ch 17.

Rnd 1: sc in 2nd ch from hook, sc 2, 2 sc in next 2 sts, sc 6, 2 sc in next 2 sts, sc 2, 2 sc in last st, working on the other side of the foundation ch, sc 2, 2 sc in next 2 sts, sc 6, 2 sc in next 2 sts, 3 sc [40]

Rnd 2: sc 4, (2 sc in next 2 sts, sc 8) 3 times, 2 sc in next 2 sts, sc 4 [48]

Rnd 3: 2 sc in next st, sc 22, 2 sc in next 2 sts, sc 22, 2 sc in last st [52]

Rnd 4: (2 sc in next 2 sts, sc 24) twice [56]

Rnd 5: sc 1, 2 sc in next 2 sts, sc 26, 2 sc in next 2 sts, sc 25 [60]

Rnd 6: sc 2, 2 sc in next 2 sts, sc 28, 2 sc in next 2 sts, sc 26 [64]

Rnd 7: sc in each st around [64]

Rnd 8: sc 2, (sc2tog) twice, sc 28, (sc2tog) twice, sc 26 [60]

Rnd 9: sc 1, (sc2tog) twice, sc 26, (sc2tog) twice, sc 25 [56]

Rnd 10: (sc2tog, sc2tog, sc 10) 4 times [48]

Rnd 11: (sc2tog, sc2tog, sc 8) 4 times [40]

Rnd 12: sl st in each st around [40]

Invisible fasten off (see Finishing: Invisible Fasten Off) and weave in all ends. Insert the peas into the pod.

HA-PEA CROCHETING...

Did you know there are many health benefits to crocheting? For example, relaxed repetitive motions such as the ones used in crochet can help calm down the body and the brain and thus reduce stress.

Blue is the color of trust and responsibility. The color blue can reduce stress and create feelings of calmness, relaxation, and order. Various shades of blue always work well together, like the sky meeting the ocean.

BABY BOTTLE

Materials

- 2.75mm (C/2) crochet hook
- Paintbox Yarns Cotton DK yarn: one 50g (1.75oz) ball each of Light Caramel (**tan**), Washed Teal (**teal**), and Paper White (**white**)
- 6mm safety eyes
- Scraps of **blue** and **black** yarn
- Fiberfill stuffing
- Yarn needle
- Stitch marker

Finished Size

11.5cm (4^1/$_2$in) tall by 5cm (2in) wide

Gauge

6 sc sts and 7 rows = 2.5cm (1in)

BOTTLE

Rnd 1: with **tan** yarn, sc 6 in magic loop [6]

Rnds 2-3: sc in each st around [6]

Rnd 4: 2 sc in each st around [12]

Rnds 5-6: sc in each st around [12]

Rnd 7: (sc 1, 2 sc in next st) 6 times [18]

Rnd 8: sc in each st around [18]

Rnd 9: change to **teal** yarn, working in FLO, 2 sc in each st around [36]

Rnds 10–12: working in BLO, sc in each st around [36]

Rnd 13: change to **white** yarn, working in BLO, sc2tog, sc 34 [35]

Rnd 14: (sc2tog, sc 3) 7 times [28]

Rnd 15: sc in each st around [28]

Rnd 16: 2 sc in next st, sc 27 [29]

Rnd 17: sc in each st around [29]

Rnd 18: sc 14, 2 sc in next st, sc 14 [30]

Rnd 19: sc in each st around [30]

Rnd 20: sc 7, 2 sc in next st, sc 22 [31]

Rnd 21: sc in each st around [31]

Rnd 22: sc 23, 2 sc in next st, sc 7 [32]

Rnd 23: sc in each st around [32]

Rnd 24: 2 sc in next st, sc 31 [33]

Rnd 25: sc in each st around [33]

Rnd 26: (2 sc in next st, sc 10) 3 times [36]

Rnds 27–34: sc in each st around [36]

Place 6mm safety eyes between **Rnds 25 and 26** with 4 sts in between. Begin to stuff with fiberfill.

Rnd 35: working in BLO, (sc 4, sc2tog) 6 times [30]

Rnd 36: (sc 3, sc2tog) 6 times [24]

Rnd 37: (sc 2, sc2tog) 6 times [18]

Rnd 38: (sc 1, sc2tog) 6 times [12]

Rnd 39: (sc2tog) 6 times [6]

Finish stuffing. Fasten off and leave a long yarn tail. With a yarn needle, weave the tail through FLO to close the opening.

Add stitches for the mouth and cheeks using **black** and **blue** yarn (see Making Up: Stitching Facial Details).

Begin shaping by inserting the needle from the center bottom to the center top. Insert the needle back down from the center top to slightly off the center bottom. Insert the needle from the center bottom to the center top. Pull to create an indentation in the bottom of the bottle. Finish off and weave in all ends.

Rnd 40: with **teal** yarn, and with the bottle pointing downward, working in the front loops from **Rnd 13**, sc in each st around [36]

Finish off and weave in the ends.

IT'S A BOY...

Let someone know you are expecting by using blue yarn for a boy, pink for a girl, and green or yellow if you're not yet sure about the gender.

BLUEBERRY ICE CREAM CONE

Materials

- 2.75mm (C/2) and 3.25mm (D/3) crochet hooks
- Paintbox Yarns Cotton Aran yarn: one 50g (1.75oz) ball each of Washed Teal (**teal**) and Light Caramel (**tan**)
- Paintbox Yarns Cotton DK yarn: one 50g (1.75oz) ball each of Sailor Blue (**blue**) and Grass Green (**green**)
- 7mm safety eyes
- Scraps of **pink** and **black** yarn
- Fiberfill stuffing
- Yarn needle
- Stitch marker

Finished Size

16cm (6$\frac{1}{4}$in) tall by 7.5cm (3in) wide

Gauge

5 sc sts and 6 rows = 2.5cm (1in) using Aran yarn

ICE CREAM

Rnd 1: with **3.25mm** hook and **teal** yarn, sc 6 in magic loop [6]

Rnd 2: 2 sc in each st around [12]

Rnd 3: (sc 1, 2 sc in next st) 6 times [18]

Rnd 4: (sc 2, 2 sc in next st) 6 times [24]

Rnd 5: (sc 3, 2 sc in next st) 6 times [30]

Rnd 6: (sc 4, 2 sc in next st) 6 times [36]

Rnd 7: (sc 5, 2 sc in next st) 6 times [42]

Rnds 8-14: sc in each st around [42]

Place 7mm safety eyes between **Rnds 11 and 12** with 4 sts in between. Begin to stuff with fiberfill.

Rnd 15: (sc 5, sc2tog) 6 times [36]

Rnd 16: (sc 4, sc2tog) 6 times [30]

Rnd 17: working in FLO, ch 1, (2 hdc in next st, 4 hdc in next st) 15 times [90]

Fasten off and weave in the ends.

CONE

Rnd 1: with **3.25mm** hook and **tan** yarn, sc 6 in magic loop [6]

Rnd 2: 2 sc in each st around [12]

Rnd 3: (sc 1, 2 sc in next st) 6 times [18]

Rnd 4: (sc 2, 2 sc in next st) 6 times [24]

Rnd 5: working in BLO, sc in each st around, join with sl st in first st [24]

Rnd 6: ch 1, sc in each st around, join with sl st in first st [24]

Rnd 7: ch 1, hdc in each st around, join with sl st in first st [24]

Rnds 8-11: ch 1, (fphdc, working in BLO sc 1) 12 times, join with sl st in first st [24]

Rnd 12: ch 1, sc in each st around, join with sl st in first st [24]

Rnd 13: working in FLO, ch 3, dc 2 in same st as ch 3, dc 3, (2 dc in next st, dc 3) 5 times, join with sl st in first st [30]

Rnd 14: working in BLO, ch 1, sc in each st around, join with sl st in first st [30]

Rnds 15-18: ch 1, sc in each st around, join with sl st in first st [30]

Fasten off and leave a long yarn tail for sewing the ice cream to the cone. Stuff both the cone and the ice cream with fiberfill. Working in the back loops from **Rnd 17** of the ice cream and both loops from **Rnd 18** of the cone, sew the two pieces together (see Making Up: Sewing Two Pieces Together).

Add stitches for the mouth and cheeks using **black** and **pink** yarn (see Making Up: Stitching Facial Details).

Begin shaping by inserting the needle from the center bottom to the center top. Insert the needle back down from the center top to slightly off the center bottom. Insert the needle from the center bottom to the center top. Pull to create an indentation in the bottom of the cone. Finish off and weave in all ends.

LEAF (MAKE 4)

With **2.75mm** hook and **green** yarn, ch 6.

Rnd 1: sc in 2nd ch from hook, hdc 1, dc 1, hdc 1, 3 sc in last ch, working on the other side of the foundation ch, hdc 1, dc 1, hdc 1, sc 1, sl st in beginning skipped ch st [12]

Invisible fasten off (see Finishing: Invisible Fasten Off) and weave in all ends. Attach to the top of the ice cream.

BLUEBERRY (MAKE 3)

Rnd 1: with **2.75mm** hook and **blue** yarn, sc 5 in magic loop [5]

Rnd 2: 2 sc in each st around [10]

Rnd 3: (sc 1, 2 sc in next st) 5 times [15]

Rnd 4: sc in each st around [15]

Rnd 5: (sc 1, sc2tog) 5 times [10]

Stuff with fiberfill.

Rnd 6: (sc2tog) 5 times [5]

Fasten off and leave a long yarn tail. With a yarn needle, weave the tail through FLO to close the opening, weave in the ends. Attach to the top of the ice cream.

BOWL OF CHEERIOS

Materials

- 2.75mm (C/2) crochet hook
- Paintbox Yarns Cotton DK yarn: one 50g (1.75oz) ball each of Washed Teal (**teal**), Paper White (**white**), Light Caramel (**tan**), and Seafoam Blue (**light blue**)
- 7mm safety eyes

- Scrap of **black** yarn
- Fiberfill stuffing
- Yarn needle
- Stitch marker

Finished Size

8cm (3$\frac{1}{4}$in) tall by 10cm (4in) wide

Gauge

6 sc sts and 7 rows = 2.5cm (1in)

MILK

Rnd 1: with **white** yarn, sc 6 in magic loop [6]

Rnd 2: 2 sc in each st around [12]

Rnd 3: (sc 1, 2 sc in next st) 6 times [18]

Rnd 4: (sc 2, 2 sc in next st) 6 times [24]

Rnd 5: (sc 3, 2 sc in next st) 6 times [30]

Rnd 6: (sc 4, 2 sc in next st) 6 times [36]

Rnd 7: (sc 5, 2 sc in next st) 6 times [42]

Rnd 8: (sc 6, 2 sc in next st) 6 times [48]

Rnd 9: (sc 5, 2 sc in next st) 8 times [56]

Rnd 10: (sc 6, 2 sc in next st) 8 times [64]

Rnd 11: sc in each st around [64]

Invisible fasten off (see Finishing: Invisible Fasten Off) and weave in all ends.

BOWL

Rnd 1: with **teal** yarn, sc 6 in magic loop [6]

Rnd 2: 2 sc in each st around [12]

Rnd 3: (sc 1, 2 sc in next st) 6 times [18]

Rnd 4: (sc 2, 2 sc in next st) 6 times [24]

Rnd 5: (sc 3, 2 sc in next st) 6 times [30]

Rnd 6: (sc 4, 2 sc in next st) 6 times [36]

Rnd 7: working in BLO, sc in each st around [36]

Rnd 8: sc in each st around [36]

Rnd 9: (sc2tog, sc 4) 6 times [30]

Rnd 10: (sc 2, 2 sc in next st) 10 times [40]

Rnd 11: (sc 4, 2 sc in next st) 8 times [48]

Rnd 12: (sc 5, 2 sc in next st) 8 times [56]

Rnd 13: (sc 6, 2 sc in next st) 8 times [64]

Rnds 14-20: sc in each st around [64]

Rnd 21: change to **white** yarn, sc in each st around [64]

Rnd 22: change to **teal** yarn, sc in each st around [64]

Rnd 23: change to **white** yarn, sc in each st around [64]

Place 7mm safety eyes between **Rnds 18 and 19** with 5 sts in between. Stuff with fiberfill.

Rnd 24: change to **teal** yarn, place the milk in the bowl and line up the stitches from **Rnd 23** of the bowl and **Rnd 11** of the milk. Sc around, working in both loops of both pieces to join them together (see Making Up: Crocheting Two Pieces Together), sl st in 1st sc to join [64]

Rnd 25: ch 1, sc in each st around, sl st in 1st sc to join [64]

Rnd 26: sl st in each st around [64]

Invisible fasten off and weave in ends.

Add stitches for the mouth with **black** yarn (see Making Up: Stitching Facial Details).

CHEERIO (MAKE 18)

With **tan** yarn, ch 6, sl st in first ch to make a circle.

Rnd 1: 10 sc into the circle, sl st in 1st sc to join

Fasten off and weave in the ends. Attach the cheerios to the milk.

SPOON

Rnd 1: with **light blue** yarn, sc 6 in magic loop [6]

Rnd 2: (sc 1, 2 sc in next st) 3 times [9]

Rnd 3: (sc 2, 2 sc in next st) 3 times [12]

Rnd 4: (sc 3, 2 sc in next st) 3 times [15]

Rnd 5: (sc 4, 2 sc in next st) 3 times [18]

Rnds 6-8: sc in each st around [18]

Rnd 9: (sc 4, sc2tog) 3 times [15]

Rnd 10: (sc 3, sc2tog) 3 times [12]

Rnd 11: sc in each st around [12]

Rnd 12: (sc 2, sc2tog) 3 times [9]

Rnd 13: (sc 1, sc2tog) 3 times [6]

Rnds 14-28: sc in each st around [6]

Stuff only the handle of the spoon with fiberfill. Fasten off and weave in the ends.

MILK CARTON

Materials

- 2.75mm (C/2) crochet hook

- Paintbox Yarns Cotton DK yarn: one 50g (1.75oz) ball each of Paper White (**white**) and Sailor Blue (**blue**)
- 7mm safety eyes
- Scraps of **black** and **blue** yarn
- Fiberfill stuffing
- Yarn needle
- Stitch marker

Finished Size

10cm (4in) tall by 6cm (2$\frac{1}{2}$in) wide

Gauge

6 sc sts and 7 rows = 2.5cm (1in)

CARTON

With **white** yarn, ch 13.

Row 1: sc in 2nd ch from hook, sc 11, turn [12]

Rows 2-12: ch 1, sc 12, turn [12]

You will now be working the rest of the pattern in a continuous rnd, around all 4 sides of the square.

Rnd 13: sc around all 4 sides making 11 sc sts in each side and 2 sc sts in each corner [52]

Rnd 14: working in BLO, sc in each st around [52]

Rnds 15-25: sc in each st around [52]

Rnd 26: change to **blue** yarn, sc in each st around [52]

Rnds 27-30: sc in each st around [52]

Place 7mm safety eyes between **Rnds 21 and 22** with 4 sts in between. Begin to stuff with fiberfill.

Rnd 31: (sc 13, working in BLO sc 13) twice [52]

Rnd 32: sc in each st around [52]

Rnd 33: sc 13, (2 sc in next st, sc 1) 6 times, 2 sc in next st, sc 13, (2 sc in next st, sc 1) 6 times, 2 sc in last st [66]

Rnd 34: sc in each st around [66]

Rnd 35: sc 13, (sc 2, 2 sc in next st) 6 times, sc 15, (sc 2, 2 sc in next st) 6 times, sc 2 [78]

Rnds 36-39: sc in each st around [78]

Finish stuffing (1). Fold in the sides where the BLO stitches were made (2).

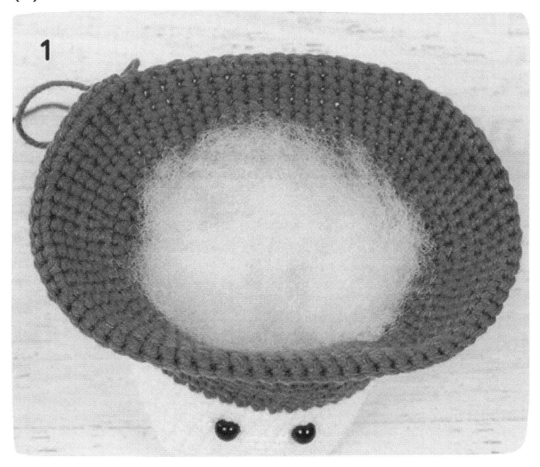

With **blue** yarn, sew the center stitches together (3).

Fasten off and weave in the ends. Fold the remaining two sides together. Join the **white** yarn in the top right corner and sc across, working in the stitches of both sides to join them together (4).

Turn work, ch 1, sc in each st across, turn work, sl st in each st across. Fasten off and weave in the ends.

Add stitches for the mouth and cheeks using **black** and **blue** yarn (see Making Up: Stitching Facial Details). Add the word 'milk' in **white** yarn on the front of the carton (5).

Begin shaping by inserting the yarn needle with **white** yarn from the center bottom to the center top (under the milk flaps), insert needle back down from the center top to slightly off the center bottom. Insert the needle from the center bottom to the center top. Pull to create an indentation in the bottom of the milk carton. Finish off and weave in the ends.

RAIN CLOUD

Materials

- 2.75mm (C/2) crochet hook
- Paintbox Yarns Cotton DK yarn: one 50g (1.75oz) ball each of Seafoam Blue (**light blue**) and Sailor Blue (**dark blue**)
- 7mm safety eyes
- Scraps of **dark blue** and **black** yarn
- Fiberfill stuffing
- Yarn needle
- Stitch marker

Finished Size

14cm (5$\frac{1}{2}$in) tall by 13cm (5in) wide

Gauge

6 sc sts and 7 rows = 2.5cm (1in)

CLOUD

Rnd 1: with **light blue** yarn, sc 6 in magic loop [6]

Rnd 2: 2 sc in each st around [12]

Rnd 3: (sc 1, 2 sc in next st) 6 times [18]

Rnd 4: (sc 2, 2 sc in next st) 6 times [24]

Rnds 5-8: sc in each st around [24]

Rnd 9: sc 9, (sc2tog, sc 1) 3 times, sc 6 [21]

Rnd 10: sc 8, (2 sc in next st, sc 1) 4 times, sc 5 [25]

Rnd 11: sc 8, (2 sc in next st, sc 2) 4 times, sc 5 [29]

Rnd 12: sc 12, 2 sc in next st, sc 3, 2 sc in next st, sc 12 [31]

Rnd 13: sc 9, hdc 15, sc 7 [31]

Rnd 14: sc 13, hdc 9, sc 9 [31]

Rnds 15-16: sc in each st around [31]

Rnd 17: sc 14, (sc2tog, sc 1) 3 times, sc 8 [28]

Rnd 18: sc 13, (2 sc in next st, sc 1) 4 times, sc 7 [32]

Rnd 19: sc 14, (2 sc in next st, sc 2) 4 times, sc 6 [36]

Rnd 20: sc 18, 2 sc in next st, sc 3, 2 sc in next st, sc 13 [38]

Rnd 21: sc 18, 2 sc in next st, sc 4, 2 sc in next st, sc 14 [40]

Rnd 22: sc 16, hdc 12, sc 12 [40]

Rnd 23: sc 19, hdc 7, sc 14 [40]

Rnd 24: sc in each st around [40]

Rnd 25-26: sc 16, hdc 12, sc 12 [40]

Rnd 27: sc in each st around [40]

Rnd 28: sc 20, hdc 7, sc 13 [40]

Rnd 29: sc 18, hdc 12, sc 10 [40]

Rnd 30: sc 20, sc2tog, sc 4, sc2tog, sc 12 [38]

Place 7mm safety eyes between **Rnds 22 and 23** for one eye and **Rnds 27 and 28** for the second eye. Begin to stuff with fiberfill.

Rnd 31: sc 20, sc2tog, sc 3, sc2tog, sc 11 [36]

Rnd 32: sc 14, (sc2tog, sc 2) 4 times, sc 6 [32]

Rnd 33: sc 14, (sc2tog, sc 1) 4 times, sc 6 [28]

Rnd 34: sc 14, (sc2tog) 4 times, sc 6 [24]

Rnd 35: (sc 2, sc2tog) 6 times [18]

Rnd 36: (sc 1, sc2tog) 6 times [12]

Rnd 37: (sc2tog) 6 times [6]

Finish stuffing. Fasten off and leave a long yarn tail. With a yarn needle, weave the tail through FLO to close the opening. Weave in all ends.

Add stitches for the mouth and cheeks using **black** and **dark blue** yarn (see Making Up: Stitching Facial Details).

RAINDROP (MAKE 3)

Rnd 1: with **dark blue** yarn, sc 5 in magic loop [5]

Rnd 2: 2 sc in each st around [10]

Rnd 3: (sc 1, 2 sc in next st) 5 times [15]

Rnds 4-5: sc in each st around [15]

Rnd 6: (sc 3, sc2tog) 3 times [12]

Stuff with fiberfill.

Rnd 7: (sc 2, sc2tog) 3 times [9]

Rnd 8: sc in each st around [9]

Rnd 9: (sc 1, sc2tog) 3 times [6]

Fasten off and leave a long yarn tail. With a yarn needle, weave the tail through FLO to close the opening. Weave in all ends.

With **light blue** yarn, attach the raindrops to the bottom of the cloud in **Rnds 10, 18, and 26**. Hang the middle raindrop 4cm (1^1/$_2$in) from the cloud and the other two raindrops 2.5cm (1in) from the cloud. Fasten off and weave in ends.

Purple is a color full of presence and one that can stimulate the imagination. It's a strong color that can be a bit tricky when incorporating it into a design. A surefire way to use it successfully is to employ it monochromatically—that is with other shades of the same color.

BEET

Materials

- 3.25mm (D/3) crochet hook
- Paintbox Yarns Cotton Aran yarn: one 50g (1.75oz) ball each of Pansy Purple (**purple**) and Grass Green (**green**)
- 7mm safety eyes
- Scraps of **pink** and **black** yarn
- Fiberfill stuffing
- Yarn needle
- Stitch marker

Finished Size

18cm (7in) tall by 8.5cm (3$\frac{1}{4}$in) wide

Gauge

5 sc sts and 6 rows = 2.5cm (1in)

BEET

Rnd 1: with **purple** yarn, sc 6 in magic loop [6]

Rnd 2: sc in each st around [6]

Rnd 3: (sc 1, 2 sc in next st) 3 times [9]

Rnd 4: (sc 2, 2 sc in next st) 3 times [12]

Rnd 5: (sc 1, 2 sc in next st) 6 times [18]

Rnd 6: (sc 2, 2 sc in next st) 6 times [24]

Rnd 7: (sc 3, 2 sc in next st) 6 times [30]

Rnd 8: (sc 4, 2 sc in next st) 6 times [36]

Rnd 9: (sc 5, 2 sc in next st) 6 times [42]

Rnd 10: (sc 6, 2 sc in next st) 6 times [48]

Rnds 11-15: sc in each st around [48]

Rnd 16: (sc 3, sc2tog, sc 3) 6 times [42]

Rnd 17: (sc 5, sc2tog) 6 times [36]

Place 7mm safety eyes between **Rnds 13 and 14** with 5 sts in between. Begin to stuff with fiberfill.

Rnd 18: (sc 2, sc2tog, sc 2) 6 times [30]

Rnd 19: (sc 3, sc2tog) 6 times [24]

Rnd 20: (sc 1, sc2tog, sc 1) 6 times [18]

Rnd 21: (sc2tog, sc 1) 6 times [12]

Rnd 22: (sc2tog) 6 times [6]

Finish stuffing. Fasten off and leave a long yarn tail. With a yarn needle, weave the tail through FLO to close the opening. Weave in all ends.

Add stitches for the mouth and cheeks using **black** and **pink** yarn (see Making Up: Stitching Facial Details).

LEAF (MAKE 3)

With **purple** yarn, ch 16.

Row 1: sc in 2nd ch from hook, sc 4, change to **green** yarn, sc 1, hdc 1, dc 2, hdc 1, sc 1, hdc 1, dc 2, 6 dc in next st, working on the other side of the foundation ch, dc 2, hdc 1, sc 1, hdc 1, dc 2, hdc 1, sc 1, change to **purple** yarn, sl st 5

Fasten off and leave a long yarn tail. Sew the leaves to the top of the beet using the yarn tail and a yarn needle.

Beet Leaf Chart

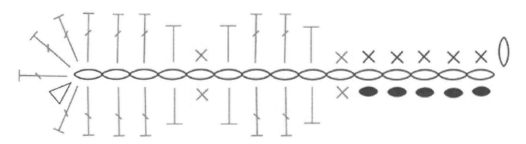

HOT AIR BALLOON

Materials

- 2.75mm (C/2) crochet hook
- Paintbox Yarns Cotton DK yarn: one 50g (1.75oz) ball each of Pansy Purple (**purple**), Paper White (**white**), and Light Caramel (**tan**)
- 7mm safety eyes
- Scraps of **black** and **pink** yarn
- Fiberfill stuffing
- Yarn needle
- Stitch marker

Finished Size

15cm (6in) tall by 8cm ($3^1/4$in) wide

Gauge

6 sc sts and 7 rows = 2.5cm (1in)

BALLOON

Rnd 1: with **purple** yarn, sc 6 in magic loop [6]

Rnd 2: 2 sc in each st around [12]

You will now be crocheting using 2 strands of yarn in each rnd, one of each color (see Colorwork: Carrying Yarn / Crocheting with Two

Colors).

Rnd 3: (change to **white** yarn, sc 1, 2 sc in next st, change to **purple** yarn, sc 1, 2 sc in next st) 3 times [18]

Rnd 4: (change to **white** yarn, sc 2, 2 sc in next st, change to **purple** yarn, sc 2, 2 sc in next st) 3 times [24]

Rnd 5: (change to **white** yarn, sc 3, 2 sc in next st, change to **purple** yarn, sc 3, 2 sc in next st) 3 times [30]

Rnd 6: (change to **white** yarn, sc 4, 2 sc in next st, change to **purple** yarn, sc 4, 2 sc in next st) 3 times [36]

Rnd 7: (change to **white** yarn, sc 5, 2 sc in next st, change to **purple** yarn, sc 5, 2 sc in next st) 3 times [42]

Rnd 8: (change to **white** yarn, sc 6, 2 sc in next st, change to **purple** yarn, sc 6, 2 sc in next st) 3 times [48]

Rnds 9-16: (change to **white** yarn, sc 8, change to **purple** yarn, sc 8) 3 times [48]

Place 7mm safety eyes between **Rnds 13 and 14** with 4 sts in between. Begin to stuff with fiberfill.

Rnd 17: (change to **white** yarn, sc 6, sc2tog, change to **purple** yarn, sc 6, sc2tog) 3 times [42]

Rnd 18: (change to **white** yarn, sc 5, sc2tog, change to **purple** yarn, sc 5, sc2tog) 3 times [36]

Rnd 19: (change to **white** yarn, sc 4, sc2tog, change to **purple** yarn, sc 4, sc2tog) 3 times [30]

Rnd 20: (change to **white** yarn, sc 5, change to **purple** yarn, sc 3, sc2tog) 3 times [27]

Rnd 21: (change to **white** yarn, sc 3, sc2tog, change to **purple** yarn, sc 4) 3 times [24]

Rnd 22: (change to **white** yarn, sc 4, change to **purple** yarn, sc 2, sc2tog) 3 times [21]

Rnd 23: (change to **white** yarn, sc 4, change to **purple** yarn, sc 3) 3 times [21]

Rnd 24: (change to **white** yarn, sc 2, sc2tog, change to **purple** yarn, sc 3) 3 times [18]

Rnd 25-26: (change to **white** yarn, sc 3, change to **purple** yarn, sc 3) 3 times [18]

Rnd 27: change to **white** yarn, working in BLO, (sc2tog, sc 1) 6 times [12]

Rnd 28: (sc2tog) 6 times [6]

Finish stuffing. Fasten off and leave a long yarn tail. With a yarn needle, weave the tail through FLO to close the opening. Weave in all ends.

Add stitches for the mouth and cheeks with **black** and **pink** yarn (see Making Up: Stitching Facial Details).

BASKET

Rnd 1: with **tan** yarn, sc 6 in magic loop [6]

Rnd 2: 2 sc in each st around [12]

Rnd 3: (sc 1, 2 sc in next st) 6 times [18]

Rnd 4: working in BLO, sc in each st around, sl st in 1st sc to join [18]

Rnd 5: ch 1, hdc in each st around, sl st in 1st st to join [18]

Rnd 6-7: ch 1, (fphdc, working in BLO, sc 1) 9 times, sl st in 1st st to join [18]

Rnd 8: ch 1, sc in each st around [18]

Invisible fasten off (see Finishing: Invisible Fasten Off) and weave in all ends.

With **tan** yarn, sl st in a st from **Rnd 8** of the basket, ch 6, sl st in a front loop from **Rnd 27** of the balloon to create a rope that attaches the basket to the balloon. Fasten off and weave in the ends. Make two more ropes in the same way, making sure to space them evenly.

TOAST WITH JAM

Materials

- 3.25mm (D/3) crochet hook
- Paintbox Yarns Cotton Aran yarn: one 50g (1.75oz) ball each of Pansy Purple (**purple**), Light Caramel (**tan**), and Soft Fudge (**brown**)
- 8mm safety eyes
- Scraps of **pink** and **black** yarn
- Fiberfill stuffing
- Yarn needle
- Stitch marker

Finished Size

10cm (4in) tall by 9cm ($3^{1}/_{2}$in) wide

Gauge

5 sc sts and 6 rows = 2.5cm (1in)

TOAST (MAKE 2)

With **tan** yarn, ch 15.

Row 1: sc in 2nd ch from hook, sc 13, turn [14]

Rows 2-16: ch 1, sc in each st across, turn [14]

Row 17: ch 1, 6 sc in 1st st, sc 12, 6 sc in last st [24]

Rnd 18: working around the entire piece, sc 15, 2 sc in the corner, sc 14, 2 sc in the corner, sc 15, (sc 1, 2 sc in next st) 3 times, sc 12, (2 sc in next st, sc 1) 3 times [78]

Rnd 19: change to **brown** yarn, sc 16, 2 sc in next st, sc 14, 2 sc in next st, sc 46 [80]

Invisible fasten off (see Finishing: Invisible Fasten Off) and weave in all ends. Do not cut the yarn and weave in the ends on the second piece of toast.

JAM

With **purple** yarn, ch 9.

Row 1: sc in 2nd ch from hook, sc 7, turn [8]

Rows 2-11: ch 1, sc in each st across, turn [8]

Rnd 12: working around the entire piece, 2 sc in first st, sc 9, 2 sc in the corner, sc 8, 2 sc in the corner, sc 9, 2 sc in the corner, sc 8 [42]

Rnd 13: hdc 1, 4 hdc in next st, hdc 1, sl st 1, skip next st, 6 hdc in next st, skip next st, sl st 2, hdc 1, 4 hdc in next st, 4 hdc in next st, hdc 1, sl st 3, sc 1, hdc 1, 4 hdc in next st, hdc 1, sc 1, sl st 2, skip next st, 6 hdc in next st, skip next st, sl st 3, sc 1, hdc 1, 4 hdc in next st, hdc 1, sc 1, sl st 3, hdc 1, 4 hdc in next st, hdc 1, sl st 2 [66]

Invisible fasten off and weave in all ends.

Place jam on top of the second piece of toast. Place 8mm safety eyes between **Rnds 4 and 5** of the jam and between **Rnds 7 and 8** of the toast with 4 sts in between.

Attach the jam to the toast. Place the first piece of toast, with right side facing out, underneath the second piece of toast. With the yarn used to make the second piece of toast, sl st around both pieces of toast, joining them together. Stuff lightly with fiberfill as you go. Fasten off and weave in the ends.

Add stitches for the mouth and cheeks using **black** and **pink** yarn (see Making Up: Stitching Facial Details).

TURNIP

Materials

- 3.25mm (D/3) crochet hook
- Paintbox Yarns Cotton Aran yarn: one 50g (1.75oz) ball each of Champagne White (**cream**), Tea Rose (**purple**) and Grass Green (**green**)
- 7mm safety eyes
- Scraps of **purple** and **black** yarn
- Fiberfill stuffing
- Yarn needle
- Stitch marker

Finished Size

18cm (7in) tall by 9cm (3$\frac{1}{2}$in) wide

Gauge

5 sc sts and 6 rows = 2.5cm (1in)

TURNIP

Rnd 1: with **cream** yarn, sc 6 in magic loop [6]

Rnd 2: sc in each st around [6]

Rnd 3: (sc 1, 2 sc in next st) 3 times [9]

Rnd 4: (sc 2, 2 sc in next st) 3 times [12]

Rnd 5: (sc 1, 2 sc in next st) 6 times [18]

Rnd 6: (sc 2, 2 sc in next st) 6 times [24]

Rnd 7: (sc 3, 2 sc in next st) 6 times [30]

Rnd 8: (sc 4, 2 sc in next st) 6 times [36]

Rnd 9: (sc 5, 2 sc in next st) 6 times [42]

Rnd 10: (sc 6, 2 sc in next st) 6 times [48]

Rnd 11: (sc 15, 2 sc in next st) 3 times [51]

Rnds 12-15: sc in each st around [51]

Rnd 16: change to **purple** yarn, sc in each st around [51]

Rnd 17: (sc2tog, sc 15) 3 times [48]

Rnd 18: (sc 3, sc2tog, sc 3) 6 times [42]

Rnd 19: (sc 5, sc2tog) 6 times [36]

Place 7mm safety eyes between **Rnds 13 and 14** with 5 sts in between. Begin to stuff with fiberfill.

Rnd 20: (sc 2, sc2tog, sc 2) 6 times [30]

Rnd 21: (sc 3, sc2tog) 6 times [24]

Rnd 22: (sc 1, sc2tog, sc 1) 6 times [18]

Rnd 23: (sc2tog, sc 1) 6 times [12]

Rnd 24: (sc2tog) 6 times [6]

Finish stuffing. Fasten off and leave a long yarn tail. With a yarn needle, weave the tail through FLO to close the opening. Weave in all ends.

Add stitches for the mouth and cheeks using **black** and **purple** yarn (see Making Up: Stitching Facial Details).

LEAF (MAKE 3)

With **green** yarn, ch 16.

Row 1: sc in 2nd ch from hook, sc 5, hdc 1, dc 2, hdc 1, sc 1, hdc 1, dc 2, 6 dc in next st, working on the other side of the foundation ch, dc 2, hdc 1, sc 1, hdc 1, dc 2, hdc 1, sc 1, sl st 5

Fasten off and leave a long yarn tail. Sew the leaves to the top of the turnip using the yarn tail and a yarn needle.

Turnip Leaf Chart

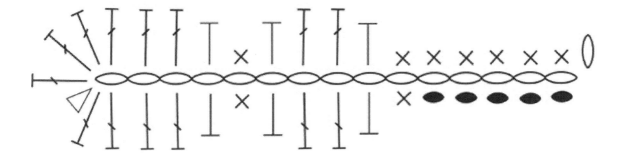

WEDDING CAKE

Materials

- 3.25mm (D/3) crochet hook
- Paintbox Yarns Cotton Aran yarn: one 50g (1.75oz) ball each of Paper White (**white**), Pansy Purple (**purple**), and Tea Rose (**pink**)
- 7mm safety eyes
- Scraps of **pink** and **black** yarn
- Fiberfill stuffing
- Yarn needle
- Stitch marker

Finished Size

13cm (5in) tall by 9cm (3$\frac{1}{2}$in) wide

Gauge

5 sc sts and 6 rows = 2.5cm (1in)

BOTTOM TIER OF CAKE

Rnd 1: with **white** yarn, sc 6 in magic loop [6]

Rnd 2: 2 sc in each st around [12]

Rnd 3: (sc 1, 2 sc in next st) 6 times [18]

Rnd 4: (sc 2, 2 sc in next st) 6 times [24]

Rnd 5: (sc 3, 2 sc in next st) 6 times [30]

Rnd 6: (sc 4, 2 sc in next st) 6 times [36]

Rnd 7: (sc 5, 2 sc in next st) 6 times [42]

Rnd 8: (sc 6, 2 sc in next st) 6 times [48]

Rnd 9: working in BLO, sc in each st around [48]

Rnds 10-17: sc in each st around [48]

Place 7mm safety eyes between **Rnds 11 and 12** with 4 sts in between. Begin to stuff with fiberfill.

Rnd 18: working in BLO (sc 6, sc2tog) 6 times [42]

Rnd 19: (sc 5, sc2tog) 6 times [36]

Rnd 20: (sc 4, sc2tog) 6 times [30]

Rnd 21: (sc 3, sc2tog) 6 times [24]

Rnd 22: (sc 2, sc2tog) 6 times [18]

Rnd 23: (sc 1, sc2tog) 6 times [12]

Rnd 24: (sc2tog) 6 times [6]

Finish stuffing. Fasten off and leave a long yarn tail. With a yarn needle, weave the tail through FLO to close the opening. Weave in all ends.

Add stitches for the eyelashes, mouth, and cheeks using **black** and **pink** yarn (see Making Up: Stitching Facial Details).

TOP TIER OF CAKE

Rnd 1: with **white** yarn, sc 6 in magic loop [6]

Rnd 2: 2 sc in each st around [12]

Rnd 3: (sc 1, 2 sc in next st) 6 times [18]

Rnd 4: (sc 2, 2 sc in next st) 6 times [24]

Rnd 5: (sc 3, 2 sc in next st) 6 times [30]

Rnd 6: (sc 4, 2 sc in next st) 6 times [36]

Rnd 7: working in BLO, sc in each st around [36]

Rnds 8-13: sc in each st around [36]

Rnd 14: working in BLO, (sc 4, sc2tog) 6 times [30]

Rnd 15: (sc 3, sc2tog) 6 times [24]

Rnd 16: (sc 2, sc2tog) 6 times [18]

Stuff with fiberfill.

Rnd 17: (sc 1, sc2tog) 6 times [12]

Rnd 18: (sc2tog) 6 times [6]

Fasten off and leave a long yarn tail. With a yarn needle, weave the tail through FLO to close the opening. Weave in all ends.

Sew the top tier to the bottom tier.

Begin shaping by inserting the needle from the center bottom to the center top. Insert the needle back down from the center top to slightly off the center bottom. Insert the needle from the center bottom to the center top. Pull to create an indentation in the bottom tier of the cake. Finish off and weave in all ends.

FROSTING FOR BOTTOM TIER OF CAKE (MAKE 2)

Row 1: with **purple** yarn (ch 4, 5-dc-bl (see Special Stitches: 5-Double Crochet Bobble) in 4th ch from hook) 13 times, ch 1 [13 bobble sts]

Fasten off and weave in the ends. Attach to the edge (one at the bottom and one at the top) of the bottom tier of cake.

FROSTING FOR TOP TIER OF CAKE

Row 1: with **purple** yarn (ch 4, 5-dc-bl (see Special Stitches: 5-Double Crochet Bobble) in 4th ch from hook) 10 times, ch 1 [10 bobble sts]

Fasten off and weave in the ends. Attach to the top edge of the top tier of cake.

FLOWER (MAKE 3)

Rnd 1: with **pink** yarn, sc 6 in magic loop [6]

Rnd 2: working in BLO, (sl st + ch 2 + 3 dc + ch 2 + sl st 1 all in same st) 6 times [6 petals]

Fasten off and weave in all ends. Attach the flowers to the top of the cake.

PiNK

Pink is the sweeter version of red.
It is cute, romantic, caring, and
playful. The color pink represents
nurturing and unconditional love.
It is also a sign of hope; inspiring
comfortable feelings and a sense
that everything will be okay.

COTTON CANDY

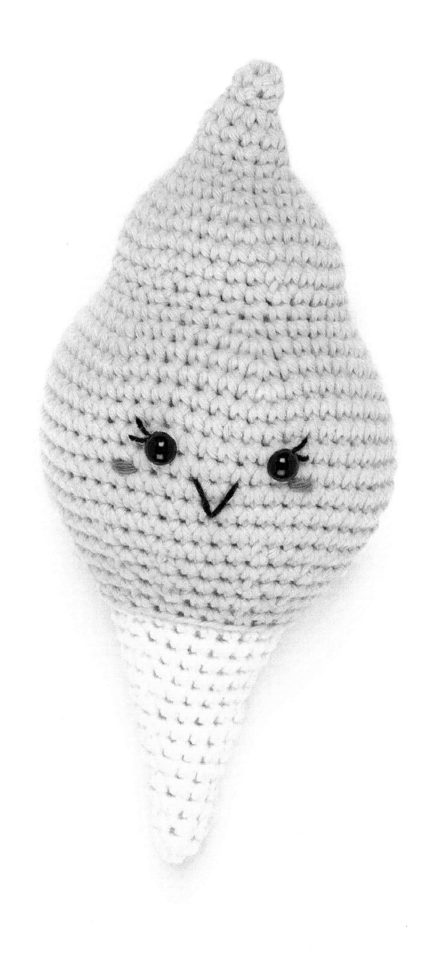

Materials

- 3.25mm (D/3) crochet hook
- Paintbox Yarns Cotton Aran yarn: one 50g (1.75oz) ball each of Candyfloss Pink (**pink**) and Paper White (**white**)
- 8mm safety eyes
- Scraps of **dark pink** and **black** yarn
- Fiberfill stuffing
- Yarn needle
- Stitch marker

Finished Size

21.5cm (8$^1/_2$in) tall by 10cm (4in) wide

Gauge

5 sc sts and 6 rows = 2.5cm (1in)

COTTON CANDY

Rnd 1: with **pink** yarn, sc 6 in magic loop [6]

Rnds 2-3: sc in each st around [6]

Rnd 4: 2 sc in each st around [12]

Rnds 5-6: sc in each st around [12]

Rnd 7: (sc 1, 2 sc in next st) 6 times [18]

Rnd 8: sc in each st around [18]

Rnd 9: (sc 2, 2 sc in next st) 6 times [24]

Rnd 10: (sc 3, 2 sc in next st) 6 times [30]

Rnd 11: (sc 4, 2 sc in next st) 6 times [36]

Rnds 12-13: sc in each st around [36]

Rnd 14: (sc 4, sc2tog) 6 times [30]

Rnd 15: sc in each st around [30]

Rnd 16: (sc 4, 2 sc in next st) 6 times [36]

Rnd 17: (sc 5, 2 sc in next st) 6 times [42]

Rnd 18: (sc 6, 2 sc in next st) 6 times [48]

Rnd 19: (sc 7, 2 sc in next st) 6 times [54]

Rnds 20-26: sc in each st around [54]

Place 8mm safety eyes between **Rnds 21 and 22** with 5 sts in between. Begin to stuff with fiberfill.

Rnd 27: (sc 7, sc2tog) 6 times [48]

Rnd 28: (sc 6, sc2tog) 6 times [42]

Rnd 29: (sc 5, sc2tog) 6 times [36]

Rnd 30: (sc 4, sc2tog) 6 times [30]

Rnd 31: (sc 3, sc2tog) 6 times [24]

Rnd 32: change to **white** yarn, working in BLO, sc in each st around [24]

Rnd 33: (sc 6, sc2tog) 3 times [21]

Rnd 34: sc in each st around [21]

Rnd 35: (sc 5, sc2tog) 3 times [18]

Rnd 36: sc in each st around [18]

Rnd 37: (sc 4, sc2tog) 3 times [15]

Rnd 38: sc in each st around [15]

Rnd 39: (sc 3, sc2tog) 3 times [12]

Rnd 40: sc in each st around [12]

Rnd 41: (sc 2, sc2tog) 3 times [9]

Rnd 42: sc in each st around [9]

Rnd 43: (sc 1, sc2tog) 3 times [6]

Rnd 44: sc in each st around [6]

Finish stuffing. Fasten off and leave a long yarn tail. With a yarn needle, weave the tail through FLO to close the opening. Weave in all ends.

Add stitches for the eyelashes, mouth, and cheeks using **black** and **dark pink** yarn (see Making Up: Stitching Facial Details).

SWEETLY SPUN...

Give one as a Valentine's gift. Simply attach a tag that says, "Valentine, you're sweet as candy, and I've cotton to like you a lot!"

HEART

Materials

- 2.75mm (C/2) crochet hook
- Paintbox Yarns Cotton DK yarn: one 50g (1.75oz) ball in Bubblegum Pink (**pink**)
- 7mm safety eyes
- Scraps of **red** and **black** yarn
- Fiberfill stuffing
- Yarn needle
- Stitch marker

Finished Size

10cm (4in) tall by 10cm (4in) wide

Gauge

6 sc sts and 7 rows = 2.5cm (1in)

HEART

Rnd 1: with **pink** yarn, sc 6 in magic loop [6]

Rnd 2: 2 sc in each st around [12]

Rnd 3: (sc 1, 2 sc in next st) 6 times [18]

Rnd 4: (sc 2, 2 sc in next st) 6 times [24]

Rnd 5: (sc 3, 2 sc in next st) 6 times [30]

Rnd 6: (sc 4, 2 sc in next st) 6 times [36]

Rnds 7-11: sc in each st around [36]

Invisible fasten off (see Finishing: Invisible Fasten Off) and weave in all ends.

Repeat **rnds 1-11**, but do not fasten off the second piece.

Place the first piece in front of the second piece (1). Join them together with a sc st in the next 6 sts (2).

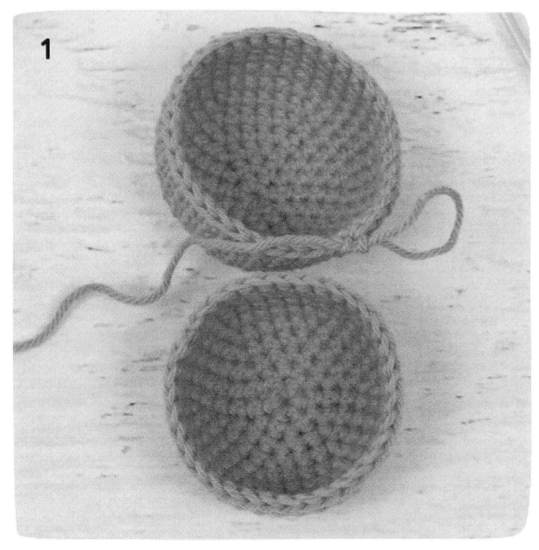

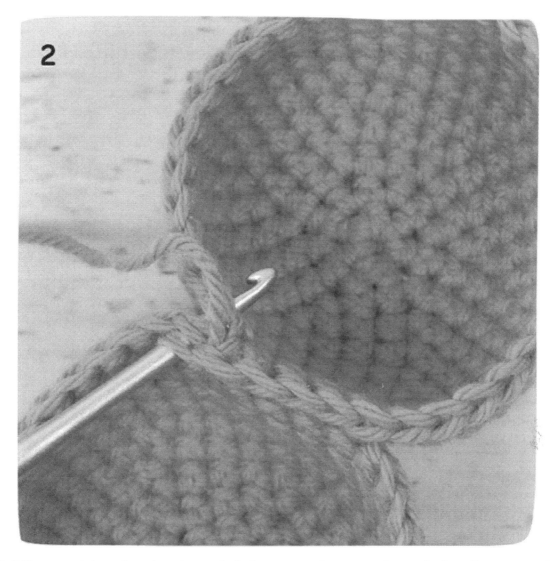

Rnd 12: working in the last joining st of piece 2 and the first st of piece 2, sc2tog (3).

Continue working around piece 2, sc 28 (4), working in the last st of piece 2 and the first joining st of piece 2, sc2tog (5).

Working in the first joining st of piece 1 and the first st of piece 1, sc2tog, continue working around piece 1, sc 28, working in the last st of piece 1 and the last joining st of piece 1, sc2tog [60]

Rnd 13: (sc 8, sc2tog) 6 times [54]

Rnd 14: sc in each st around [54]

Rnd 15: (sc 7, sc2tog) 6 times [48]

Rnd 16: sc in each st around [48]

Rnd 17: (sc 6, sc2tog) 6 times [42]

Rnd 18: sc in each st around [42]

Rnd 19: (sc 5, sc2tog) 6 times [36]

Rnd 20: sc in each st around [36]

Place 7mm safety eyes between **Rnds 17 and 18** with 5 sts in between. Begin to stuff with fiberfill.

Rnd 21: (sc 4, sc2tog) 6 times [30]

Rnd 22: sc in each st around [30]

Rnd 23: (sc 3, sc2tog) 6 times [24]

Rnd 24: sc in each st around [24]

Rnd 25: (sc 2, sc2tog) 6 times [18]

Rnd 26: sc in each st around [18]

Rnd 27: (sc 1, sc2tog) 6 times [12]

Rnd 28: sc in each st around [12]

Rnd 29: (sc2tog) 6 times [6]

Finish stuffing. Fasten off and leave a long yarn tail. With a yarn needle, weave the tail through FLO to close the opening. Weave in all ends.

Add stitches for the mouth and cheeks using **black** and **red** yarn (see Making Up: Stitching Facial Details).

SO BIG HEARTED...

Make a heart pillow by using a Super Bulky weight yarn instead (you will need 310g). The finished pillow will measure 30.5cm (12in) tall by 24cm (9$\frac{1}{2}$in) wide.

STRAWBERRY ICE CREAM CONE

Materials

- 2.75mm (C/2) and 3.25mm (D/3) crochet hooks
- Paintbox Yarns Cotton Aran yarn: one 50g (1.75oz) ball each of Candyfloss Pink (**light pink**), Light Caramel (**tan**), and Paper White (**white**)
- Paintbox Yarns Cotton DK yarn: one 50g (1.75oz) ball each of Bubblegum Pink (**dark pink**) and Lime Green (**lime**)
- 7mm safety eyes
- Scraps of **pink** and **black** yarn
- Fiberfill stuffing
- Yarn needle
- Stitch marker

Finished Size

16.5cm (6$^1/_2$in) tall by 7.5cm (3in) wide

Gauge

5 sc sts and 6 rows = 2.5cm (1in) using Aran yarn

ICE CREAM

Rnd 1: with **3.25mm** hook and **light pink** yarn, sc 6 in magic loop [6]

Rnd 2: 2 sc in each st around [12]

Rnd 3: (sc 1, 2 sc in next st) 6 times [18]

Rnd 4: (sc 2, 2 sc in next st) 6 times [24]

Rnd 5: (sc 3, 2 sc in next st) 6 times [30]

Rnd 6: (sc 4, 2 sc in next st) 6 times [36]

Rnd 7: (sc 5, 2 sc in next st) 6 times [42]

Rnds 8-14: sc in each st around [42]

Place 7mm safety eyes between **Rnds 11 and 12** with 4 sts in between. Begin to stuff with fiberfill.

Rnd 15: (sc 5, sc2tog) 6 times [36]

Rnd 16: (sc 4, sc2tog) 6 times [30]

Rnd 17: working in FLO ch 1, (2 hdc in next st, 4 hdc in next st) 15 times [90]

Fasten off and weave in the ends.

CONE

Rnd 1: with **3.25mm** hook and **tan** yarn, sc 6 in magic loop [6]

Rnd 2: 2 sc in each st around [12]

Rnd 3: (sc 1, 2 sc in next st) 6 times [18]

Rnd 4: (sc 2, 2 sc in next st) 6 times [24]

Rnd 5: working in BLO, sc in each st around, join with sl st in first st [24]

Rnd 6: ch 1, sc in each st around, join with sl st in first st [24]

Rnd 7: ch 1, hdc in each st around, join with sl st in first st [24]

Rnds 8-11: ch 1, (fphdc, working in BLO sc 1) 12 times, join with sl st in first st [24]

Rnd 12: ch 1, sc in each st around, join with sl st in first st [24]

Rnd 13: working in FLO, ch 3, dc 2 in same st as ch 3, dc 3, (2 dc in next st, dc 3) 5 times, join with sl st in first st [30]

Rnd 14: working in BLO, ch 1, sc in each st around, join with sl st in first st [30]

Rnds 15-18: ch 1, sc in each st around, join with sl st in first st [30]

Fasten off and leave a long yarn tail for sewing the ice cream to the cone. Stuff both the cone and the ice cream with fiberfill. Working in the back loops from **Rnd 17** of the ice cream and both loops from **Rnd 18** of the cone, sew the two pieces together (see Making Up: Sewing Two Pieces Together)

Add stitches for the mouth and cheeks using **black** and **pink** yarn (see Making Up: Stitching Facial Details).

Begin shaping by inserting the needle from the center bottom to the center top. Insert the needle back down from the center top to slightly off the center bottom. Insert the needle from the center bottom to the center top. Pull to create an indentation in the bottom of the cone. Finish off and weave in all ends.

WHIPPED CREAM

Rnd 1: with **3.25mm** hook and **white** yarn, sc 6 in magic loop [6]

Rnd 2: 2 sc in each st around [12]

Rnd 3: (sc 1, 2 sc in next st) 6 times [18]

Rnd 4: (sc 2, 2 sc in next st) 6 times [24]

Rnd 5: 3 hdc in each st around [72]

Invisible fasten off (see Finishing: Invisible Fasten Off) and weave in all ends. Attach whipped cream to the top of the ice cream.

STRAWBERRY

Rnd 1: with **2.75mm** hook and **dark pink** yarn, sc 6 in magic loop [6]

Rnd 2: (sc 1, 2 sc in next st) 6 times [9]

Rnd 3: (sc 2, 2 sc in next st) 6 times [12]

Rnd 4: (sc 3, 2 sc in next st) 6 times [15]

Rnd 5: (sc 4, 2 sc in next st) 6 times [18]

Rnd 6: sc in each st around [18]

Rnd 7: (sc 1, sc2tog) 6 times [12]

Stuff with fiberfill.

Rnd 8: (sc2tog) 6 times [6]

Fasten off and leave a long yarn tail. With a yarn needle, weave the tail through FLO to close the opening. Weave in all ends. Attach to the center of the whipped cream.

STEM

With **2.75mm** hook and **lime** yarn, ch 4, sl st in 1st ch to form a circle.

Rnd 1: (ch 6, sl st into the circle) 6 times

Fasten off and attach to the top of the strawberry.

BOWL OF FRUIT LOOPS

Materials

- 2.75mm (C/2) crochet hook
- Paintbox Yarns Cotton DK yarn: one 50g (1.75oz) ball each of Bubblegum Pink (**pink**), Paper White (**white**), Blush Pink (**light pink**), and any shade of **red**, **orange**, **yellow**, **green**, **blue**, and **purple**
- 7mm safety eyes
- Scrap of **black** yarn
- Fiberfill stuffing
- Yarn needle

- Stitch marker

Finished Size

8cm (3$\frac{1}{4}$in) tall by 10cm (4in) wide

Gauge

6 sc sts and 7 rows = 2.5cm (1in)

MILK

Rnd 1: with **white** yarn, sc 6 in magic loop [6]

Rnd 2: 2 sc in each st around [12]

Rnd 3: (sc 1, 2 sc in next st) 6 times [18]

Rnd 4: (sc 2, 2 sc in next st) 6 times [24]

Rnd 5: (sc 3, 2 sc in next st) 6 times [30]

Rnd 6: (sc 4, 2 sc in next st) 6 times [36]

Rnd 7: (sc 5, 2 sc in next st) 6 times [42]

Rnd 8: (sc 6, 2 sc in next st) 6 times [48]

Rnd 9: (sc 5, 2 sc in next st) 8 times [56]

Rnd 10: (sc 6, 2 sc in next st) 8 times [64]

Rnd 11: sc in each st around [64]

Invisible fasten off (see Finishing: Invisible Fasten Off) and weave in all ends.

BOWL

Rnd 1: with **pink** yarn, sc 6 in magic loop [6]

Rnd 2: 2 sc in each st around [12]

Rnd 3: (sc 1, 2 sc in next st) 6 times [18]

Rnd 4: (sc 2, 2 sc in next st) 6 times [24]

Rnd 5: (sc 3, 2 sc in next st) 6 times [30]

Rnd 6: (sc 4, 2 sc in next st) 6 times [36]

Rnd 7: working in BLO, sc in each st around [36]

Rnd 8: sc in each st around [36]

Rnd 9: (sc2tog, sc 4) 6 times [30]

Rnd 10: (sc 2, 2 sc in next st) 10 times [40]

Rnd 11: (sc 4, 2 sc in next st) 8 times [48]

Rnd 12: (sc 5, 2 sc in next st) 8 times [56]

Rnd 13: (sc 6, 2 sc in next st) 8 times [64]

Rnds 14-23: sc in each st around [64]

Place 7mm safety eyes between **Rnds 18 and 19** with 5 sts in between. Stuff with fiberfill.

Rnd 24: place the milk in the bowl and line up the stitches from **Rnd 23** of the bowl and **Rnd 11** of the milk. With the same **pink** yarn used to make the bowl, sc around working in both loops of both pieces to join them together (see Making Up: Crocheting Two Pieces Together), sl st in 1st sc to join [64]

Rnd 25: ch 1, sc in each st around, sl st in 1st sc to join [64]

Rnd 26: sl st in each st around [64]

Invisible fasten off and weave in all ends.

Add stitches for the mouth with **black** yarn (see Making Up: Stitching Facial Details).

FRUIT LOOPS (MAKE 18)

With **red** yarn, ch 6, sl st in first ch to form a circle.

Rnd 1: 10 sc into the circle, sl st in 1st sc to join [10]

Fasten off and weave in all ends.

Make three fruit loops in each of the following colors: **red**, **orange**, **yellow**, **green**, **blue**, and **purple**. Attach them to the milk.

SPOON

Rnd 1: with **light pink** yarn, sc 6 in magic loop [6]

Rnd 2: (sc 1, 2 sc in next st) 3 times [9]

Rnd 3: (sc 2, 2 sc in next st) 3 times [12]

Rnd 4: (sc 3, 2 sc in next st) 3 times [15]

Rnd 5: (sc 4, 2 sc in next st) 3 times [18]

Rnds 6-8: sc in each st around [18]

Rnd 9: (sc 4, sc2tog) 3 times [15]

Rnd 10: (sc 3, sc2tog) 3 times [12]

Rnd 11: sc in each st around [12]

Rnd 12: (sc 2, sc2tog) 3 times [9]

Rnd 13: (sc 1, sc2tog) 3 times [6]

Rnds 14-28: sc in each st around [6]

Stuff only the handle of the spoon with fiberfill. Fasten off and weave in the ends.

WATERMELON POPSICLE

Materials

- 2.75mm (C/2) crochet hook
- Paintbox Yarns Cotton DK yarn: one 50g (1.75oz) ball each of Bubblegum Pink (**pink**), Lime Green (**lime**), Grass Green (**green**), Paper White (**white**), Light Caramel (**tan**), and Pure Black (**black**)
- 7mm safety eyes
- Scraps of **red** and **black** yarn
- Fiberfill stuffing
- Yarn needle
- Stitch marker

Finished Size

14cm (5$\frac{1}{2}$in) tall by 5cm (2in) wide

Gauge

6 sc sts and 7 rows = 2.5cm (1in)

POPSICLE

Rnd 1: with **pink** yarn, sc 6 in magic loop [6]

Rnd 2: 2 sc in each st around [12]

Rnd 3: (sc 1, 2 sc in next st) 6 times [18]

Rnd 4: (sc 2, 2 sc in next st) 6 times [24]

Rnd 5: (sc 3, 2 sc in next st) 6 times [30]

Rnds 6-24: sc in each st around [30]

Rnd 25: change to **white** yarn, sc in each st around [30]

Rnd 26: change to **lime** yarn, sc in each st around [30]

Rnd 27: change to **green** yarn, sc in each st around [30]

Rnd 28: sc in each st around [30]

Place 7mm safety eyes between **Rnds 19 and 20** with 4 sts in between. Begin to stuff with fiberfill.

Rnd 29: working in BLO, (sc 3, sc2tog) 6 times [24]

Rnd 30: (sc 2, sc2tog) 6 times [18]

Rnd 31: (sc 1, sc2tog) 6 times [12]

Rnd 32: change to **tan** yarn, (sc 2, sc2tog) 3 times [9]

Rnds 33-41: sc in each st around [9]

Finish stuffing. Fasten off and leave a long yarn tail. With a yarn needle, weave the tail through FLO to close the opening. Weave in all ends.

Add stitches for the mouth and cheeks using **black** and **red** yarn (see Making Up: Stitching Facial Details), and for the seeds using **black** yarn.

Brown is a serious color. It's down to earth and signifies support, stability, comfort, and structure. In color psychology, brown is honest and relates to the hardworking and the industrious who have both feet planted firmly on the ground.

CORN DOG

Materials

- 2.75mm (C/2) crochet hook
- Paintbox Yarns Cotton DK yarn: one 50g (1.75oz) ball each of Soft Fudge (**brown**), Light Caramel (**tan**), and Buttercup Yellow (**yellow**)
- 5mm safety eyes
- Scraps of **yellow** and **black** yarn
- Fiberfill stuffing
- Wooden dowel or skewer
- Yarn needle
- Stitch marker

Finished Size

15cm (6in) tall by 4cm ($1^1/_2$in) wide

Gauge

6 sc sts and 7 rows = 2.5cm (1in)

CORN DOG

Rnd 1: with **brown** yarn, sc 6 in magic loop [6]

Rnd 2: 2 sc in each st around [12]

Rnd 3: (sc 1, 2 sc in next st) 6 times [18]

Rnd 4: (sc 2, 2 sc in next st) 6 times [24]

Rnds 5-27: sc in each st around [24]

Place 5mm safety eyes between **Rnds 20 and 21** with 3 sts in between. Begin to stuff with fiberfill.

Rnd 28: (sc 2, sc2tog) 6 times [18]

Rnd 29: (sc 1, sc2tog) 6 times [12]

Rnd 30: (sc2tog) 6 times [6]

Finish stuffing.

Rnd 31: change to **tan** yarn, sc in each st around [6]

Rnds 32-40: sc in each st around [6]

Insert a wooden dowel or skewer inside the corn dog stick.

Fasten off and leave a long yarn tail. With a yarn needle, weave the tail through FLO to close the opening. Weave in all ends.

Add stitches for the mouth and cheeks using **black** and **yellow** yarn (see Making Up: Stitching Facial Details).

MUSTARD

With **yellow** yarn, ch 25.

Row 1: working in back bump loops (see Special Stitches: Back Bump), sl st in 2nd ch from hook, sl st in each st across.

Fasten off and weave in all ends. Attach to the corn dog.

PRETZEL

Materials

- 2.75mm (C/2) crochet hook
- Paintbox Yarns Cotton DK yarn: one 50g (1.75oz) ball each of Soft Fudge (**brown**) and Paper White (**white**)

- 5mm safety eyes
- Scraps of **white** and **black** yarn
- Fiberfill stuffing
- T-pins
- Yarn needle
- Stitch marker

Finished Size

10cm (4in) tall by 11.5cm (4$\frac{1}{2}$in) wide

Gauge

6 sc sts and 7 rows = 2.5cm (1in)

PRETZEL

Rnd 1: with **brown** yarn, sc 6 in magic loop [6]

Rnd 2: 2 sc in each st around [12]

Rnds 3-77: sc in each st around [12]

Place 5mm safety eyes between **Rnds 74 and 75** with 2 sts in between. Begin to stuff with fiberfill.

The end of an 11.5mm crochet hook is the perfect size for stuffing the pretzel.

Rnds 78-116: sc in each st around [12]

Rnd 117: (sc2tog, sc 2) 3 times [9]

Rnd 118: (sc2tog, sc 1) 3 times [6]

Finish stuffing. Fasten off and leave a long yarn tail.

With a yarn needle, weave the tail through FLO to close the opening. Weave in all ends.

To shape the pretzel begin with a "U" shape (1).

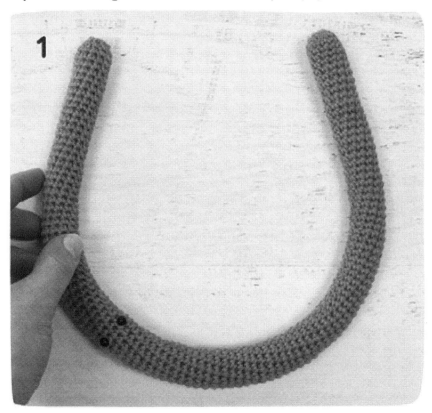

Holding the ends, cross them over each other (2).

Twist the two ends and pin onto the bottom of the "U" (3).

Secure the pretzel shape with more pins and then attach the pretzel ends together with hot glue or sew them with yarn and a yarn needle.

Add stitches for the mouth and salt using **black** and **white** yarn (see Making Up: Stitching Facial Details).

FORTUNE COOKIES

Materials

- 2.75mm (C/2) and 3.25mm (D/3) crochet hooks
- Paintbox Yarns Cotton Aran yarn: one 50g (1.75oz) ball of Light Caramel (**tan**)
- Paintbox Yarns Cotton DK yarn: one 50g (1.75oz) ball of Paper White (**white**)
- 5mm safety eyes
- Scraps of **red** and **black** yarn
- Fiberfill stuffing
- Red and pink felt

- Yarn needle
- Stitch marker

Finished Size

7.5cm (3in) tall by 4.5cm ($1\frac{3}{4}$in) wide

Gauge

5 sc sts and 6 rows = 2.5cm (1in) using Aran yarn

COOKIE

Leave a 15cm (6in) yarn tail when making the beginning slip knot.

Rnd 1: with **3.25mm** hook and **tan** yarn, sc 6 in magic ring [6]

Rnd 2: 2 sc in each st around [12]

Rnd 3: (sc 1, 2 sc in next st) 6 times [18]

Rnd 4: (sc 2, 2 sc in next st) 6 times [24]

Rnd 5: (sc 3, 2 sc in next st) 6 times [30]

Rnd 6: (sc 4, 2 sc in next st) 6 times [36]

Rnd 7: (sc 5, 2 sc in next st) 6 times [42]

Rnd 8: (sc 6, 2 sc in next st) 6 times [48]

Rnd 9: (sc 7, 2 sc in next st) 6 times [54]

Rnd 10: (sc 8, 2 sc in next st) 6 times [60]

Do not cut the yarn.

Fold the crocheted circle in half with the wrong side facing you and the last stitch made in the center. Thread a yarn needle with the beginning yarn tail. Make five or six tight stitches slightly to the side of the center (1).

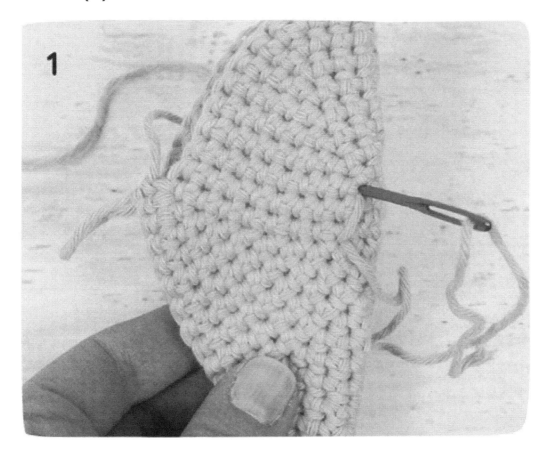

Turn the cookie so that the right sides are facing out (2).

Place 5mm safety eyes between **Rnds 6 and 7** with two stitches in between (3).

Place the eyes on one side of the cookie if making the regular version, or in the center if making the cat version.

FORTUNE

With **2.75mm** hook and **white** yarn, ch 11.

Working in back bump loops (see Special Stitches: Back Bump), sc in 2nd ch from hook, sc 9, turn.

Ch 1, sc 10, turn [10].

Ch 1, sc 10, turn [10].

Fasten off and weave in all ends.

FINISHING

Place the fortune inside the cookie with half sticking out. Begin slip stitching the two sides of the cookie together. When you get to the fortune, simply insert the hook through it as well (4 and 5).

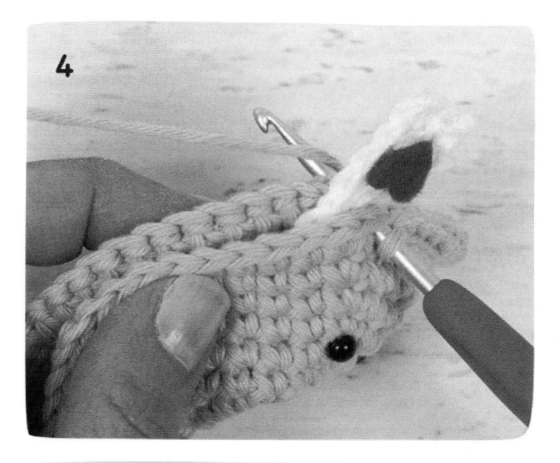

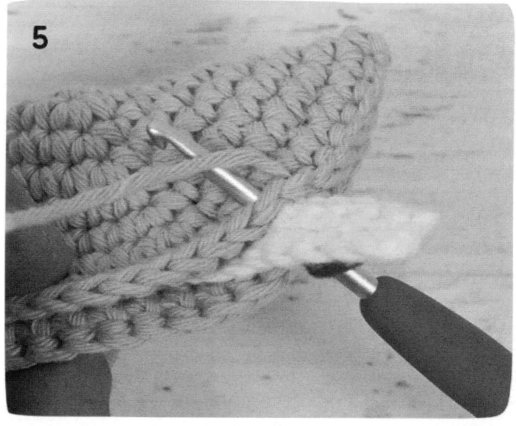

Continue slip stitching around the cookie, stuffing with fiberfill as you go. Invisible fasten off (see Finishing: Invisible Fasten Off) and weave in all ends.

Add stitches for the mouth and cheeks, or whiskers for the cat, using **black** and **red** yarn (see Making Up: Stitching Facial Details).

Cut a small heart from red felt and attach to the fortune. Cut a small triangle from pink felt and attach to the cat's nose.

302

PANCAKES

Materials

- 2.75mm (C/2) and 3.25mm (D/3) crochet hooks
- Paintbox Yarns Cotton Aran yarn: one 50g (1.75oz) ball each of Champagne White (**cream**) and Light Caramel (**tan**)
- Paintbox Yarns Cotton DK yarn: one 50g (1.75oz) ball each of Soft Fudge (**brown**) and Daffodil Yellow (**yellow**)
- 7mm safety eyes
- Scraps of **brown** and **black** yarn
- Fiberfill stuffing
- Yarn needle
- Stitch marker

Finished Size

10cm (4in) tall by 10cm (4in) wide

Gauge

5 sc sts and 6 rows = 2.5cm (1in) using Aran yarn

PANCAKE (MAKE 2)

Rnd 1: with **3.25mm** hook and **tan** yarn, sc 6 in magic loop [6]

Rnd 2: 2 sc in each st around [12]

Rnd 3: (sc 1, 2 sc in next st) 6 times [18]

Rnd 4: (sc 2, 2 sc in next st) 6 times [24]

Rnd 5: (sc 3, 2 sc in next st) 6 times [30]

Rnd 6: (sc 4, 2 sc in next st) 6 times [36]

Rnd 7: (sc 5, 2 sc in next st) 6 times [42]

Rnd 8: (sc 6, 2 sc in next st) 6 times [48]

Rnd 9: (sc 7, 2 sc in next st) 6 times [54]

Rnd 10: (sc 8, 2 sc in next st) 6 times [60]

Rnd 11: change to **cream** yarn, sc in each st around [60]

Rnd 12: sc in each st around [60]

Rnd 13: change to **tan** yarn, (sc 8, sc2tog) 6 times [54]

Rnd 14: (sc 7, sc2tog) 6 times [48]

Rnd 15: (sc 6, sc2tog) 6 times [42]

Place 7mm safety eyes between **Rnds 5 and 6** with 4 sts in between. Begin to lightly stuff with fiberfill.

Rnd 16: (sc 5, sc2tog) 6 times [36]

Rnd 17: (sc 4, sc2tog) 6 times [30]

Rnd 18: (sc 3, sc2tog) 6 times [24]

Rnd 19: (sc 2, sc2tog) 6 times [18]

Rnd 20: (sc 1, sc2tog) 6 times [12]

Rnd 21: (sc2tog) 6 times [6]

Finish stuffing. Fasten off and leave a long yarn tail. With a yarn needle, weave the tail through FLO to close the opening.

Add stitches for the mouth and cheeks using **black** and **brown** yarn (see Making Up: Stitching Facial Details).

SYRUP

Rnd 1: with **2.75mm** hook and **brown** yarn, sc 6 in magic loop [6]

Rnd 2: 2 sc in each st around [12]

Rnd 3: (sc 1, 2 sc in next st) 6 times [18]

Rnd 4: (sc 1, ch 3, hdc in 2nd ch from hook, hdc in next ch, sc in same st as ch 3, sc 1, ch 2, hdc in 2nd ch from hook, sc in same st as ch 2, sc 2, ch 4, hdc in 2nd ch from hook, hdc in next 2 ch, sc in same st as ch 4, sc 2) 3 times

Invisible fasten off (see Finishing: Invisible Fasten Off) and weave in all ends. Attach to the top of the pancake above the eyes.

BUTTER

With **2.75mm** and **yellow** yarn, ch 5.

Row 1: sc in 2nd ch from hook, sc 3, turn [4]

Rows 2-4: ch 1, sc in each st across, turn [4]

Rnd 5: sc around the entire square of butter making 4 sc sts on each side and a ch 1 at each corner [20]

Invisible fasten off and weave in all ends. Attach to the top of the syrup.

YOU MELT MY HEART...

Add different toppings using other patterns in this book. For example, the blueberries, strawberries, or cherries from the Ice Cream Cone patterns would be a delicious addition.

VANILLA ICE CREAM CONE

Materials

- 2.75mm (C/2) and 3.25mm (D/3) crochet hooks
- Paintbox Yarns Cotton Aran yarn: one 50g (1.75oz) ball each of Vanilla Cream (**cream**), Light Caramel (**tan**), and Coffee Bean (**brown Aran**)
- Paintbox Yarns Cotton DK yarn: one 50g (1.75oz) ball each of Coffee Bean (**brown DK**), and Pillar Red (**red**)
- 7mm safety eyes
- Scraps of **pink** and **black** yarn
- Fiberfill stuffing
- Yarn needle
- Stitch marker

Finished Size

18cm (7in) tall by 7.5cm (3in) wide

Gauge

5 sc sts and 6 rows = 2.5cm (1in) using Aran yarn

ICE CREAM

Rnd 1: with **3.25mm** hook and **cream** yarn, sc 6 in magic loop [6]

Rnd 2: 2 sc in each st around [12]

Rnd 3: (sc 1, 2 sc in next st) 6 times [18]

Rnd 4: (sc 2, 2 sc in next st) 6 times [24]

Rnd 5: (sc 3, 2 sc in next st) 6 times [30]

Rnd 6: (sc 4, 2 sc in next st) 6 times [36]

Rnd 7: (sc 5, 2 sc in next st) 6 times [42]

Rnds 8-14: sc in each st around [42]

Place 7mm safety eyes between **Rnds 11 and 12** with 4 sts in between. Begin to stuff with fiberfill.

Rnd 15: (sc 5, sc2tog) 6 times [36]

Rnd 16: (sc 4, sc2tog) 6 times [30]

Rnd 17: working in FLO ch 1, (2 hdc in next st, 4 hdc in next st) 15 times [90]

Fasten off and weave in the ends.

CONE

Rnd 1: with **3.25mm** hook and **tan** yarn, sc 6 in magic loop [6]

Rnd 2: 2 sc in each st around [12]

Rnd 3: (sc 1, 2 sc in next st) 6 times [18]

Rnd 4: (sc 2, 2 sc in next st) 6 times [24]

Rnd 5: working in BLO, sc in each st around, join with sl st in first st [24]

Rnd 6: ch 1, sc in each st around, join with sl st in first st [24]

Rnd 7: ch 1, hdc in each st around, join with sl st in first st [24]

Rnds 8-11: ch 1, (fphdc, working in BLO sc 1) 12 times, join with sl st in first st [24]

Rnd 12: ch 1, sc in each st around, join with sl st in first st [24]

Rnd 13: working in FLO, ch 3, dc 2 in same st as ch 3, dc 3, (2 dc in next st, dc 3) 5 times, join with sl st in first st [30]

Rnd 14: working in BLO, ch 1, sc in each st around, join with sl st in first st [30]

Rnds 15-18: ch 1, sc in each st around, join with sl st in first st [30]

Fasten off and leave a long yarn tail for sewing the ice cream to the cone. Stuff both the cone and the ice cream with fiberfill. Working in the back loops from **Rnd 17** of the ice cream and both loops from **Rnd 18** of the cone, sew the two pieces together (see Making Up: Sewing Two Pieces Together).

Add stitches for the mouth and cheeks using **black** and **pink** yarn (see Making Up: Stitching Facial Details).

Begin shaping by inserting the needle from the center bottom to the center top. Insert the needle back down from the center top to slightly off the center bottom. Insert the needle from the center bottom to the center top. Pull to create an indentation in the bottom of the cone. Finish off and weave in all ends.

CHOCOLATE

Rnd 1: with **3.25mm** hook and **brown Aran** yarn, sc 6 in magic loop [6]

Rnd 2: 2 sc in each st around [12]

Rnd 3: (sc 1, 2 sc in next st) 6 times [18]

Rnd 4: (sc 1, ch 3, hdc in 2nd ch from hook, hdc in next ch, sc in same st as ch 3, sc 1, ch 2, hdc in 2nd ch from hook, sc in same st as ch 2, sc 2, ch 4, hdc in 2nd ch from hook, hdc in next 2 ch, sc in same st as ch 4, sc 2) 3 times

Invisible fasten off (see Finishing: Invisible Fasten Off) and weave in all ends. Attach the chocolate to the top of the ice cream.

CHERRY

Rnd 1: with **2.75mm** hook and **red** yarn, sc 6 in magic loop [6]

Rnd 2: 2 sc in each st around [12]

Rnd 3: (sc 1, 2 sc in next st) 6 times [18]

Rnd 4: (sc 2, 2 sc in next st) 6 times [24]

Rnd 5: (sc 2, sc2tog) 6 times [18]

Rnd 6: (sc 1, sc2tog) 6 times [12]

Stuff with fiberfill.

Rnd 7: (sc2tog) 6 times [6]

Fasten off and leave a long yarn tail. With a yarn needle, weave the tail through FLO to close the opening. Weave in all ends. Attach to the center of the chocolate.

STEM

With **2.75mm** hook and **brown DK** yarn, ch 8.

Rnd 1: working in back bump loops (see Special Stitches: Back Bump), sc in 2nd ch from hook, sl st 6 [7]

Fasten off and attach to the top of the cherry.

YOU'RE SO COOL...

Making and giving this ice cream cone as a Valentine's gift is sure to make someone's heart melt and make you flavor of the month!

TECHNIQUES

USEFUL INFORMATION

Terminology

The patterns in this book are written using US crochet terms.

Conversion Chart (US to UK)

- Single Crochet (sc) = Double Crochet (dc)
- Double Crochet (dc) = Treble Crochet (tr)
- Half Double Crochet (hdc) = Half Treble Crochet (htr)
- Treble Crochet (tr) = Double Treble Crochet (dtr)

Pattern Abbreviations

- 5-dc-bl = 5 double crochet bobble
- 3-dc-bl = 3 double crochet bobble
- BLO = back loops only
- ch = chain stitch
- dc = double crochet stitch
- dc2tog = double crochet decrease
- FLO = front loops only
- Fphdc = front post half double crochet
- hdc = half double crochet
- hdc2tog = half double crochet decrease
- rnd = round
- sc = single crochet stitch
- sc2tog = single crochet decrease
- sl st = slip stitch
- st(s) = stitch(es)

- tr = treble crochet stitch
- yo = yarn over

Key to Pattern Charts

▷	Starting Point
𝟲	Magic Loop
⬯	Chain
⬭	Slip Stitch
✕	Single Crochet
⊤	Half Double Crochet
⊤	Double Crochet
⊤	Treble Crochet
⌒	Front Loop
⌣	Back Loop
✕✕	Single Crochet Increase

Skill Levels

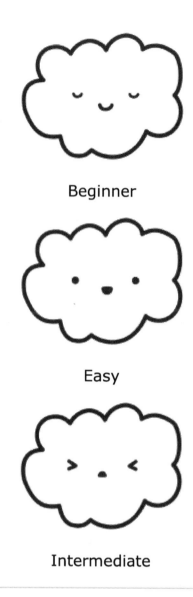

Beginner

Easy

Intermediate

How to Read Patterns

- Abbreviations are used throughout the book, please see 'Pattern Abbreviations' to see how stitches are described.
- Almost all patterns are worked in a continuous spiral; you only need to join a round if the pattern specifically instructs you to.
- If something is crocheted in rows it will begin with 'Row' instead of 'Rnd'.
- Repetitions throughout the round are placed in parentheses, and the number of times this part is repeated is added behind the parentheses. For example, **(sc 2, 2 sc in next st) 6 times**. This

means to crochet 1 single crochet stitch over the first 2 stitches, then make 2 single crochet stitches (or a single crochet increase) in the third stitch, next the sequence of 1 single crochet in the next 2 stitches and 2 single crochet stitches in the next stitch is repeated another 5 times.

- A sequence of stitches worked in the same stitch is joined with a +. For example, **(sl st + ch 2 + dc 1 + ch 2 + sl st) 4 times**. This means crochet a slip stitch, chain 2, 1 double crochet, chain 2, and a slip stitch all in the next stitch and then repeat the sequence another 3 times.
- At the end of each line you will find the total number of stitches you should have in square brackets, for example, **[24]** means you have should have 24 total stitches in that round or row once complete.

Modifying the Design

The easiest way to make your amigurumi unique is by selecting a different yarn weight to the one the pattern calls for.

For example, if you wish to make a giant Heart cushion you could use a bulky weight yarn and the amigurumi will be larger, while maintaining the same proportions. Or, if you wish to make a tiny School Pencil keychain, you could select a fingering weight yarn and a smaller hook size. The wonderful thing about amigurumi is that when the yarn weight and corresponding hook size is changed the proportions still remain the same!

If changing the yarn weight you'll need to change the hook size too. Always choose a slightly smaller hook size than the recommended size on the label band of your yarn. This helps to keep the stitches tight enough to prevent the fabric from having large stretch holes when it's stuffed.

BASIC STITCHES

Magic Loop

With the tail end of the yarn hanging down, make a loop and hold it securely between two fingers (1).

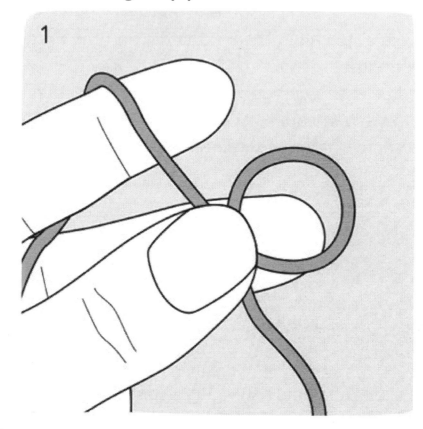

Insert the hook into the loop and pull the working yarn through (2), make a chain stitch to secure, and begin making stitches inside the loop (3). When you've finished, pull the tail to tighten the loop.

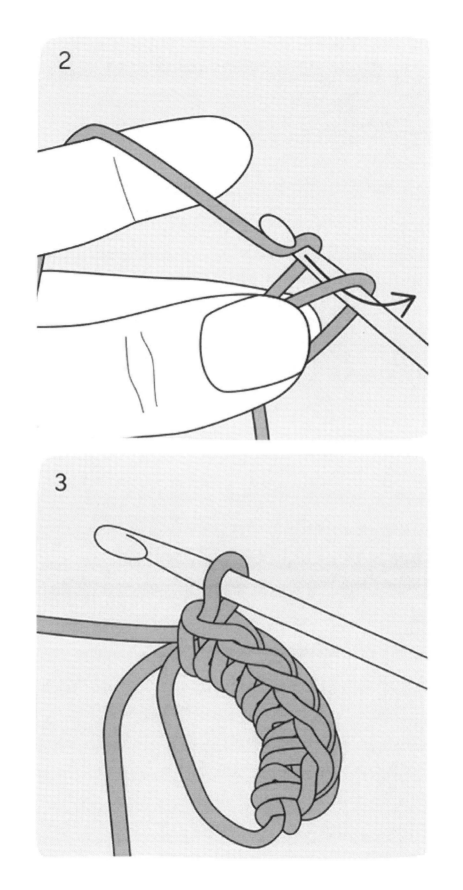

Slip Knot

Make a loop with the tail end of the yarn hanging down. Insert the hook or your fingers into the loop and pull the working yarn through (4). Pull to tighten.

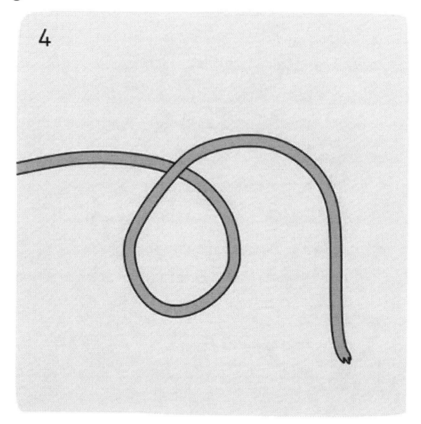

Chain (ch)

Place the yarn over the hook and pull through the loop (5).

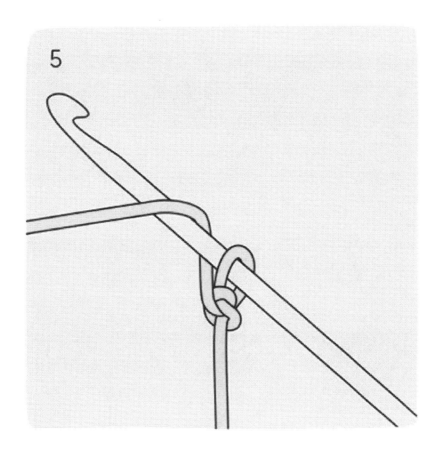

Slip Stitch (sl st)

Insert the hook into the stitch, place the yarn over the hook, and pull through the stitch (6).

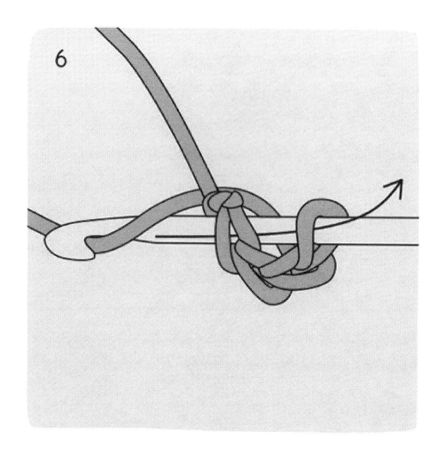

Single Crochet (sc)

Insert the hook into the stitch, place the yarn over the hook, and pull through the stitch, so that two loops are on the hook (7). Place the yarn over the hook again and pull through both loops on the hook (8).

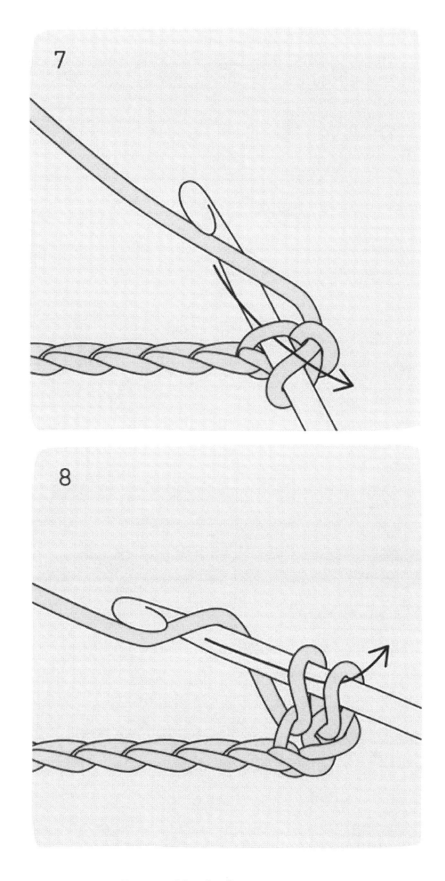

Half Double Crochet (hdc)

Place the yarn over the hook and insert the hook into the stitch (9). Yarn over and pull through the stitch. Place the yarn over the hook again and pull through all three loops on the hook (10).

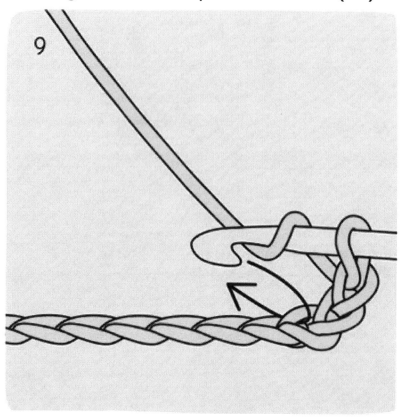

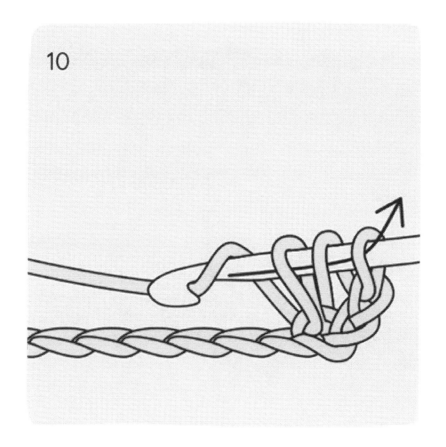

Double Crochet (dc)

Place the yarn over the hook and insert the hook into the stitch (11). Yarn over and pull through the stitch, so that three loops are left on the hook. Yarn over and pull through the first two loops on the hook, so that two loops are left on the hook (12). Yarn over and pull through the remaining two loops.

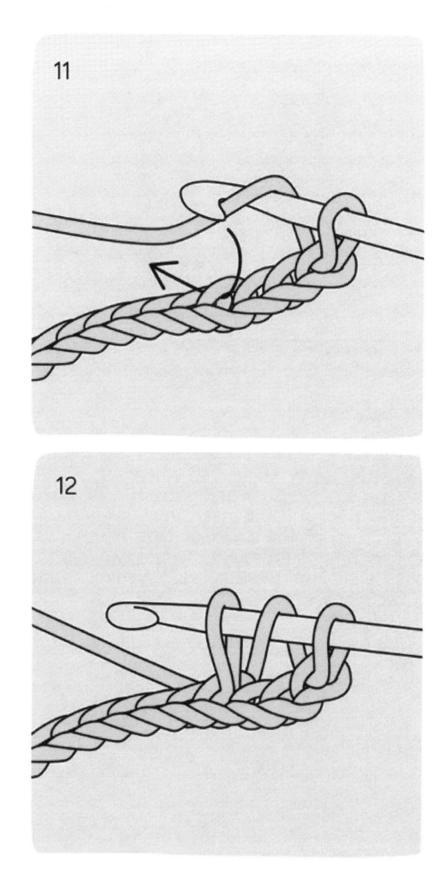

Treble Crochet (tr)

Place the yarn over the hook twice and insert the hook into the stitch (13). Yarn over and pull through the stitch. Yarn over and pull through the first two loops on the hook, so that there are three loops left on the hook (14). Yarn over and pull through the first two loops on the hook again, so that there are two loops left on the hook. Yarn over again and pull through the remaining two loops.

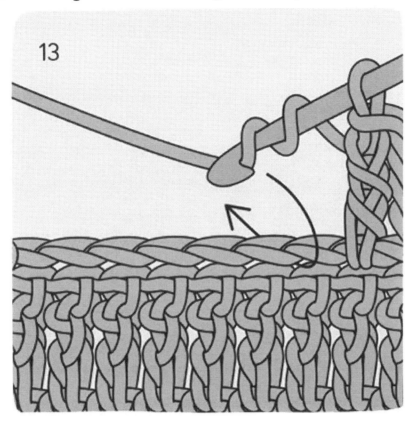

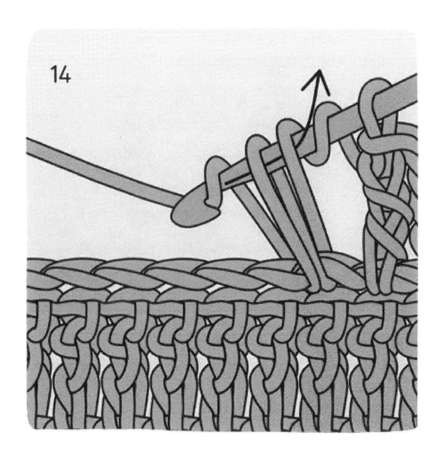

DECREASING STITCHES

Invisible Single Crochet Decrease

The standard method of decreasing can leave a small gap or bump when making a three-dimensional piece. Using the invisible single crochet decrease when making amigurumi results in a smoother and more even fabric.

Insert the hook into the front loop of the first stitch and then directly into the front loop of the second stitch, place the yarn over the hook (1), and draw the yarn through both of the front loops on your hook, two loops are now on the hook. Place the yarn over the hook again and draw the yarn through both loops on your hook to finish a single crochet stitch (2).

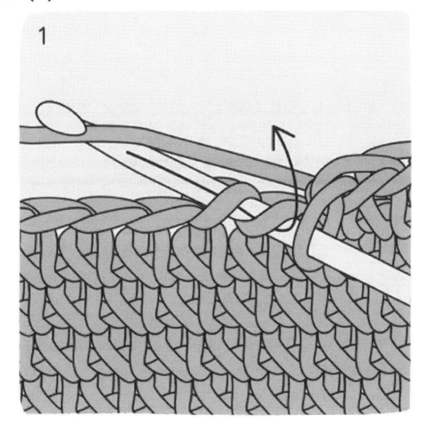

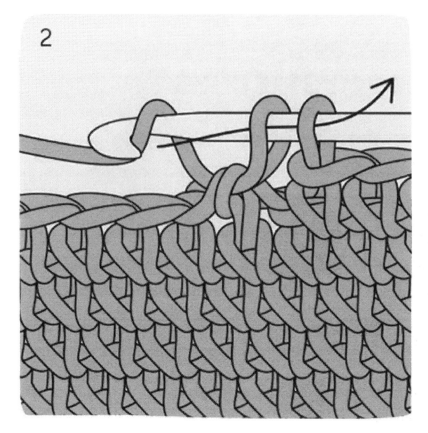

This also works for taller stitches such as hdc or dc decreases.

Standard Single Crochet Decrease (sc2tog)

Insert the hook into the first stitch, place the yarn over the hook, and pull a loop through the stitch, two loops are now on the hook (3). Insert the hook into the second stitch, place the yarn over the hook, and pull a loop through the stitch, three loops are now on the hook (4). Place the yarn over the hook and pull through all three loops on the hook.

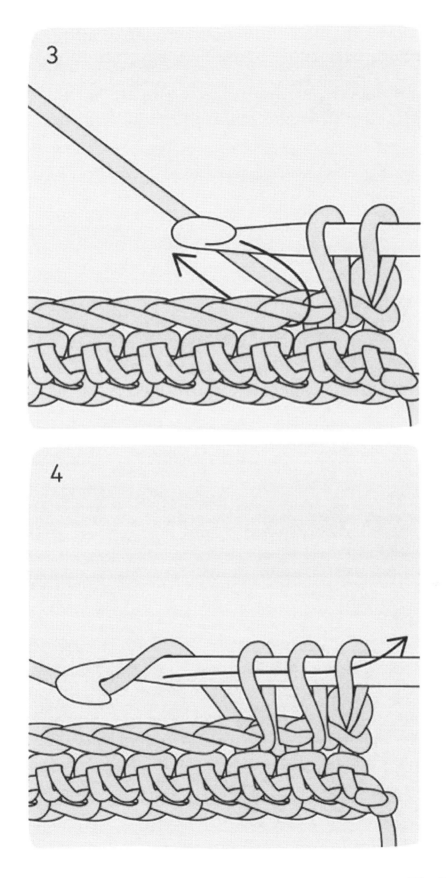

Standard Half Double Crochet Decrease (hdc2tog)

Place the yarn over the hook and insert the hook into the first stitch (5). Place the yarn over again and pull a loop through the stitch, three loops are now on the hook (6). Insert the hook into the second stitch (7). Yarn over the hook and pull through the stitch, four loops are now on the hook (8). Yarn over and pull through all four loops on the hook.

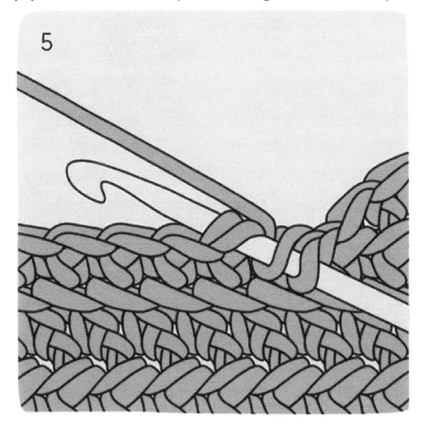

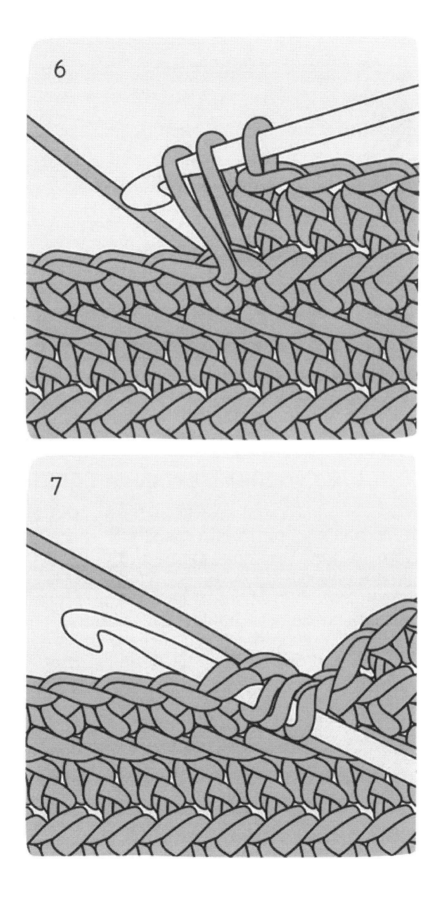

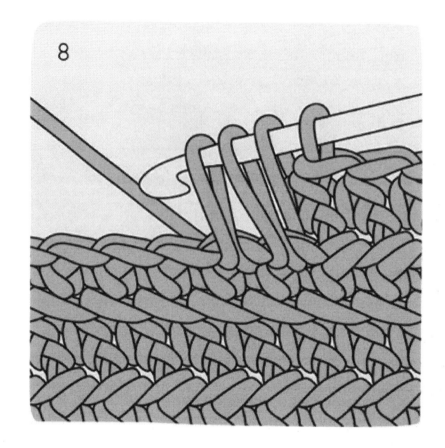

Standard Double Crochet Decrease (dc2tog)

Place the yarn over the hook and insert the hook into the first stitch (9). Yarn over and pull a loop through the stitch, three loops are now on the hook (10). Yarn over and pull through the first two loops on the hook, two loops are now on the hook (11). Yarn over and insert the hook into the second stitch (12). Yarn over and pull through the stitch, four loops are now on the hook (13). Yarn over and pull through the first two loops on the hook, three loops are now on the hook (14). Yarn over and pull through all three loops on the hook.

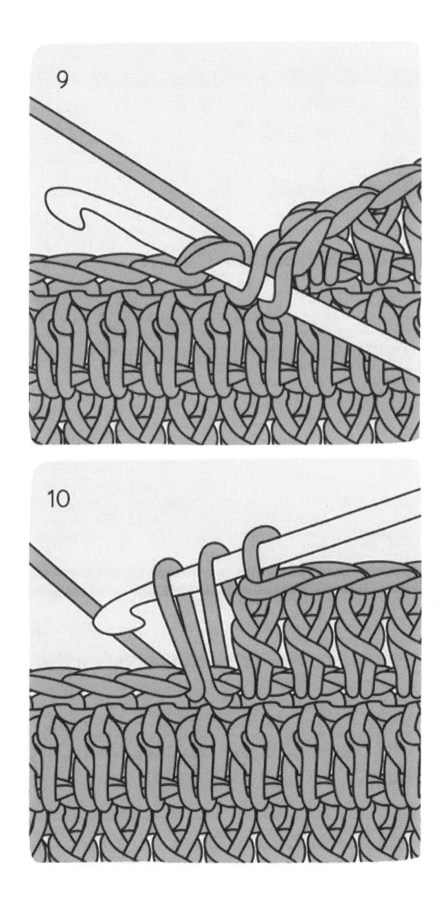

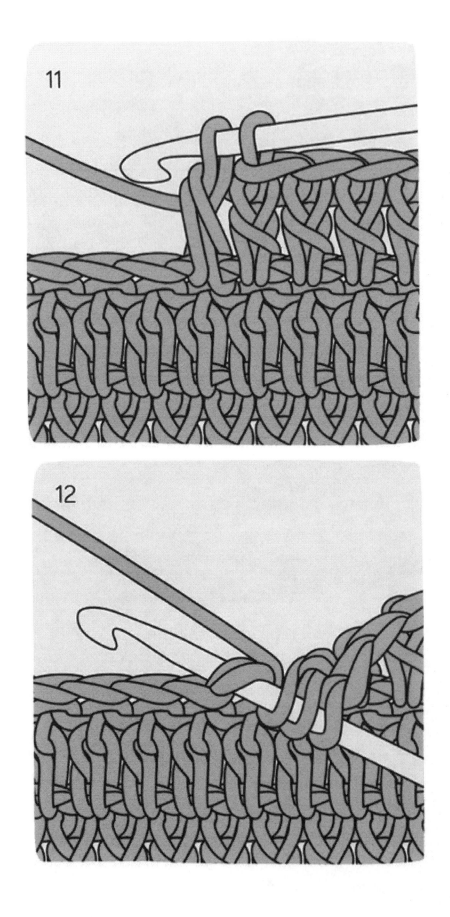

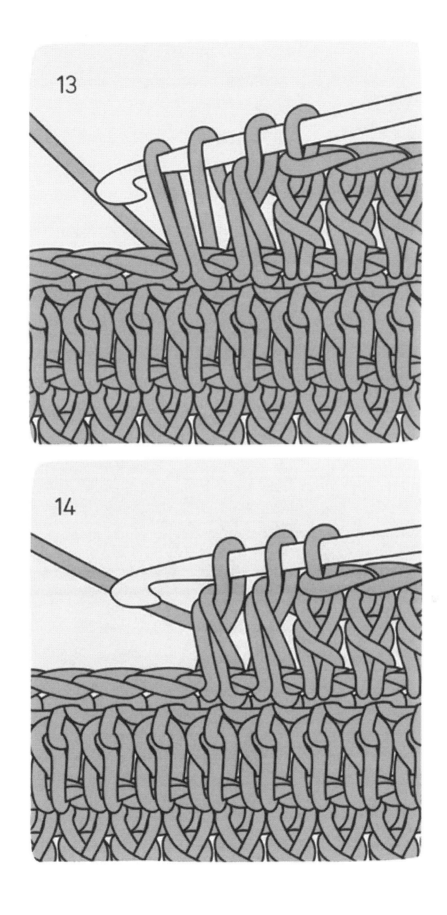

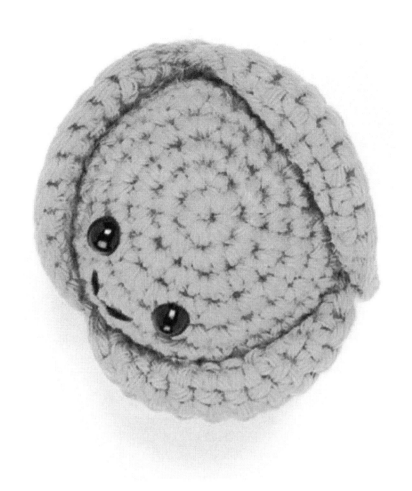

SPECIAL STITCHES

5-Double Crochet Bobble (5-dc-bl)

Place the yarn over the hook and insert the hook into the stitch, yarn over and pull the yarn through the stitch, yarn over and draw yarn through the first two loops on the hook, two loops are now on the hook.

Yarn over and insert hook into the same stitch. Yarn over and pull the yarn through the stitch. Yarn over and draw yarn through the first two loops on the hook, three loops are now on the hook.

Repeat the last step until you have six loops on the hook (1). Yarn over and pull the yarn through all six loops on the hook. Make a chain to secure the stitch (2).

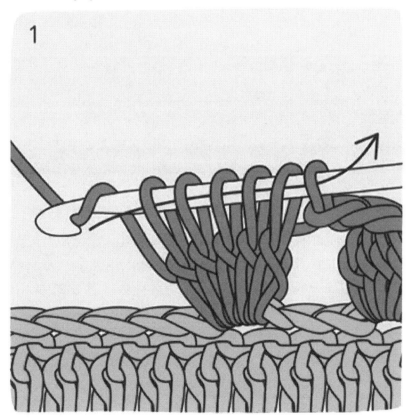

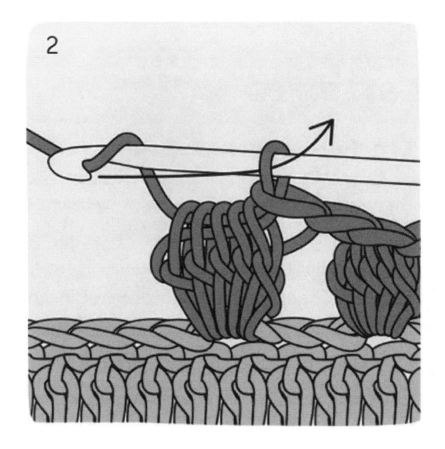

3-Double Crochet Bobble (3-dc-bl)

This is worked in the same way as a 5-Double Crochet Bobble except that you only make a total of three double crochet stitches instead of five, so in the last step you will have four loops on the hook to pull the yarn through.

Front Post Half Double Crochet (fphdc)

Place the yarn over the hook and insert the hook from front to back around the post (the upright part) of the stitch (3). Yarn over and pull up a loop, three loops are now on the hook (4). Yarn over and pull the yarn through all three loops on the hook (5).

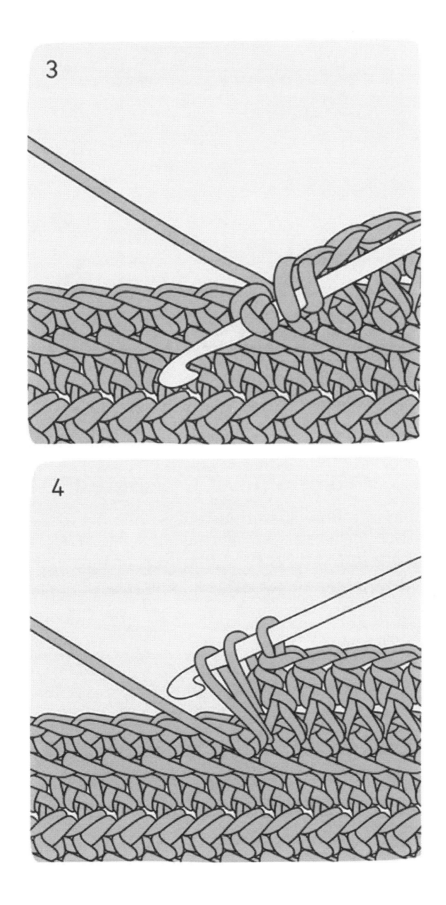

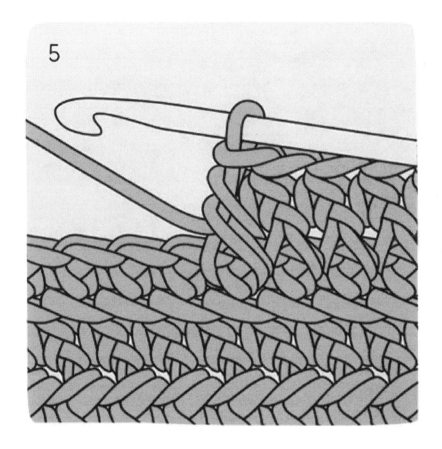

Right Side / Wrong Side of Crocheted Fabric

When crocheting in rounds it's important to be able to distinguish which side of the crocheted piece is the right side. This is especially true when you are asked to work in the front or back loops of a stitch.

On the right or front side there are little 'V's that appear (6). The wrong or back side has horizontal lines which are called back bumps or back bars (7).

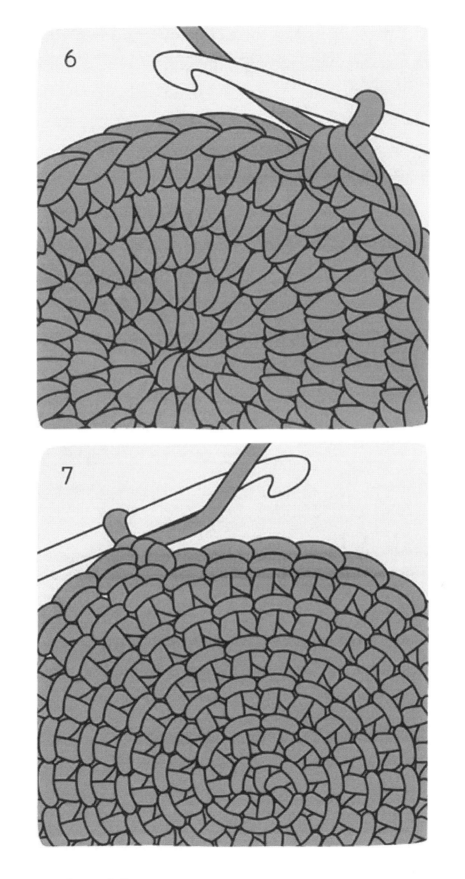

Front Loop (FLO)

The front loop of a stitch is the loop closest to you. If the crochet pattern says to work in front loops only (FLO) you will work your stitches into just this front loop (8).

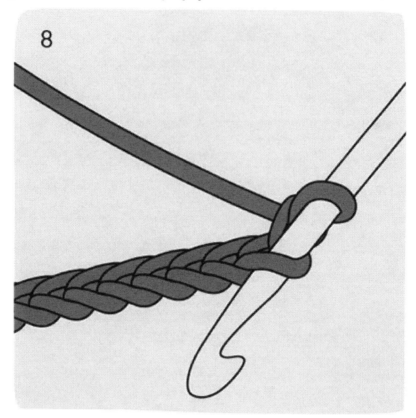

Back Loop (BLO)

The back loop is the loop furthest away from you. If the crochet pattern says to work in back loops only (BLO) you will work your stitches into just this back loop (9).

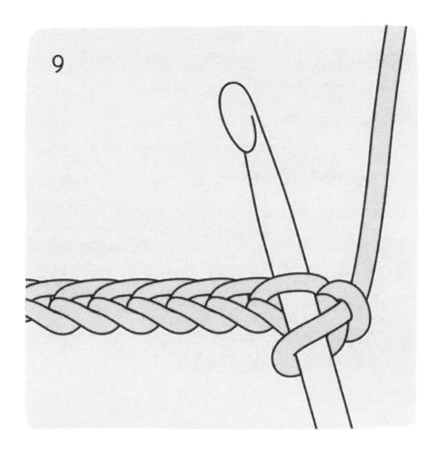

Back Bump / Back Bar

The back bump or back bar can be found on the 'wrong side' of the fabric and lies right below the back loop of a stitch (10 and 11).

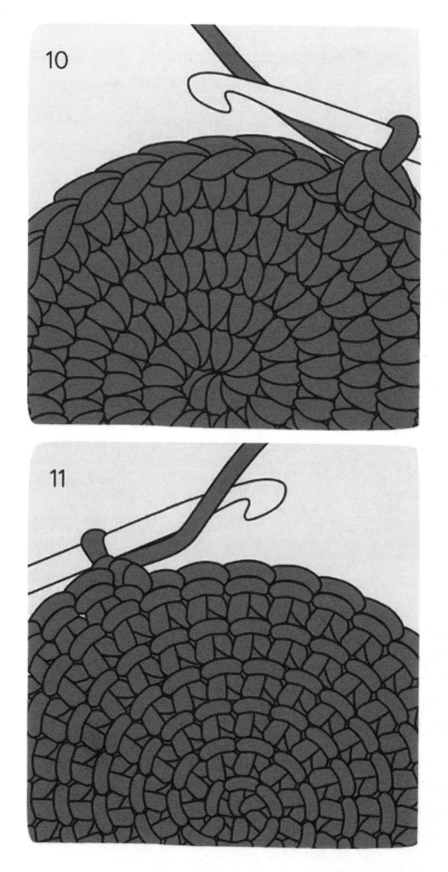

Back Bump / Back Bar of a Foundation Chain

On the front or right side of your crochet chain, the stitches are smooth and look like a series of interlocking 'V's (12). On the back or wrong side, the stitches are bumpy.

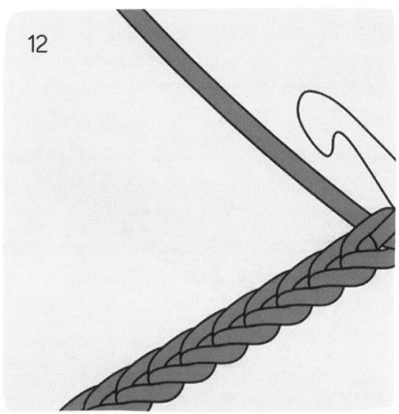

Crocheting in the back bumps along a chain creates a neater finish (13).

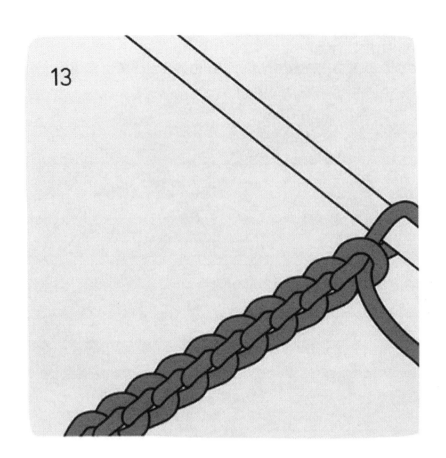

COLORWORK

Changing Colors

The color change method used throughout this book is to change the color in the last step of the previous stitch. Start the previous stitch as usual, but when completing the last yarn over pull through the new color (1). Drop the old yarn color and continue making the next stitch with the new color (2 and 3).

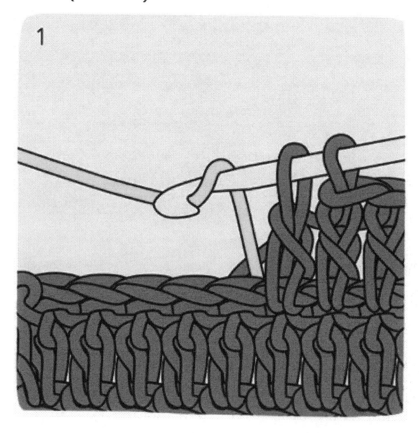

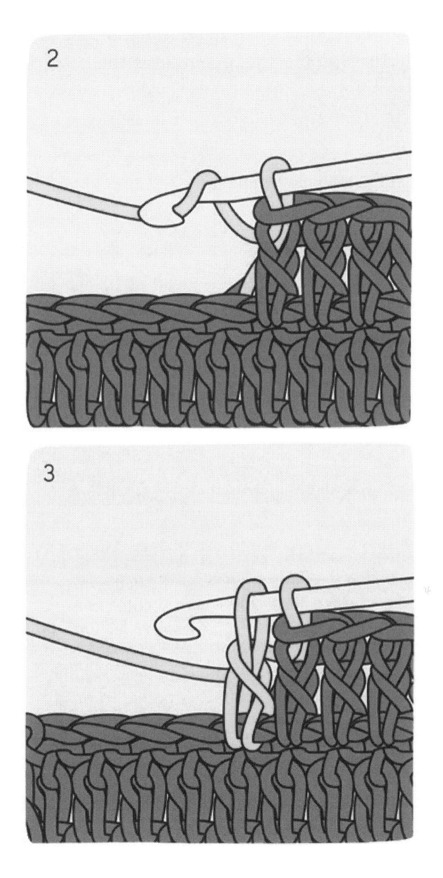

Joining Yarn

Insert the hook into the indicated stitch, wrap the yarn around the hook and pull it through the stitch, yarn over the hook, and pull through to secure (4).

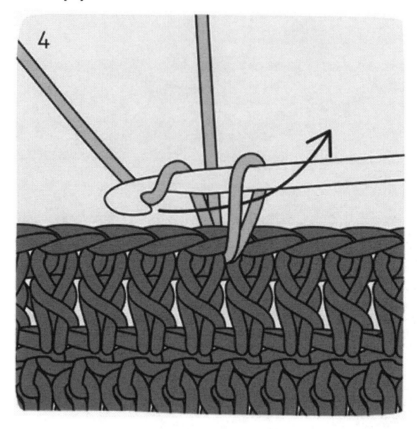

Carrying Yarn / Crocheting With Two Colors

Carrying the yarn means you don't have to fasten the yarn off and rejoin a new strand each time you make a color change. This technique is helpful when making the Hot Air Balloon pattern because a color change is made every few stitches.

There are various methods for doing this but carrying the yarn on the wrong side is the technique used in this book. To do this, you lay the unused strand of yarn across the tops of the stitches and towards the back of the previous round. Then, using the new color, work the stitches in the current round and encase the strand. Working over the carried strand produces a neat appearance on the right side of the crocheted fabric with the unused yarn peeking through the stitches on the wrong side of the fabric.

A trick that will make your color changes as seamless as possible is to change the yarn color in the last step of the previous stitch (see 'Changing Yarn Colors' technique above).

FINISHING

Fasten Off

Cut the yarn and pull the yarn tail through the last loop on your hook.

Invisible Fasten Off

When you fasten off invisibly you get a smooth even edge. Cut the yarn and pull the yarn tail through the last stitch. Thread the yarn tail onto a yarn needle, insert the needle, from front to back, into the next stitch. Now insert the needle back into the same stitch that the yarn tail is coming out of, but into the back loop only, and pull gently (5). Weave the tail end into the wrong side of the fabric and cut the excess (6).

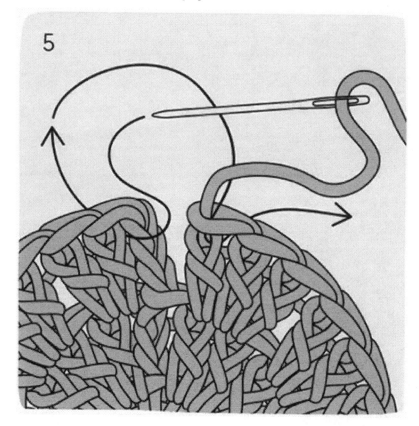

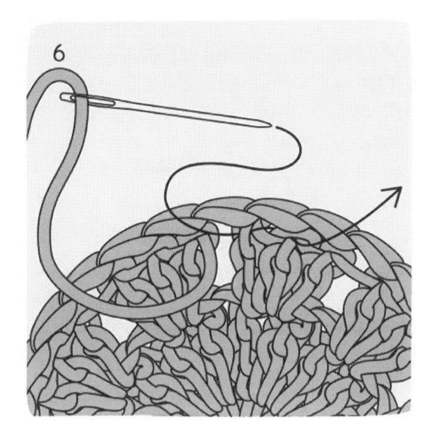

Weave In Ends As You Go

When changing colors with a three-dimensional piece, you can weave in the initial yarn tail of the new color and the remaining yarn tail of the previous color as you go by 'carrying' both yarn tails. To do this, lay both yarn tails along the edge on top of the stitches to be worked and crochet over the strands for the next five to six stitches.

MAKING UP

Inserting Safety Eyes

Safety Note: Do not use toy safety eyes if giving to a child under three years of age. Instead use black yarn to embroider the eyes.

Each pattern indicates which rows or rounds the safety eyes should be placed in and how many stitches there should be between them. Make sure you are happy with the placement of the safety eyes before inserting the washer onto the rod of the eye because once the washer is placed you won't be able to pull it off again.

Stuffing

Stuffing a piece firmly, but not so much that the stuffing shows between the stitches, is my secret to knowing how much fiberfill stuffing to use.

Closing Stitches Through Front Loops

Cut the yarn and pull the yarn tail through the last stitch. Thread onto a yarn needle. Insert the needle through the front loops only of each of the remaining stitches from inside to outside (1 and 2). Pull gently to close the hole (3). Insert the needle in the center of the stitches you just closed and come out in any direction from the middle of the crocheted piece (4). Tie a knot close to the amigurumi and push the knot inside the crocheted piece. Cut the excess yarn tail.

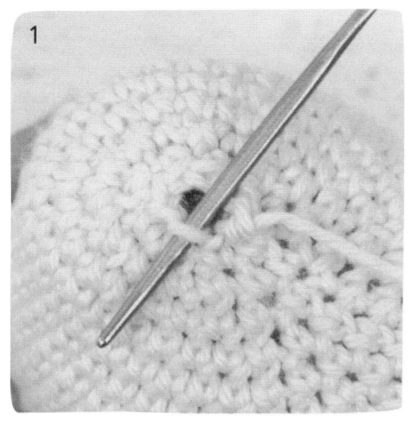

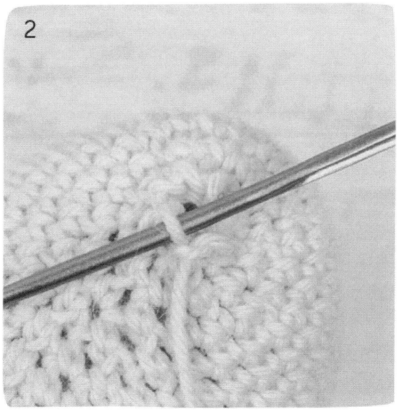

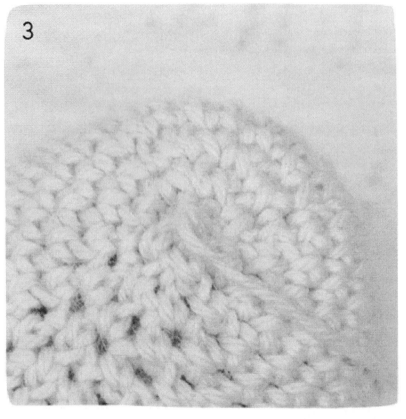

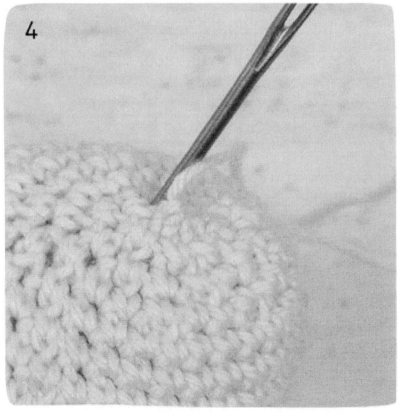

The same technique applies when closing through the back loops. You will just be inserting your needle in the back loops instead of the front loops as described.

Crocheting Two Pieces Together

Line up the stitches from both rounds that need to be crocheted together by placing one round of stitches on top of the other (5). With the yarn that has not been fastened off from one of the crochet pieces, single crochet around the entire piece working in both loops of both pieces to join them together (6).

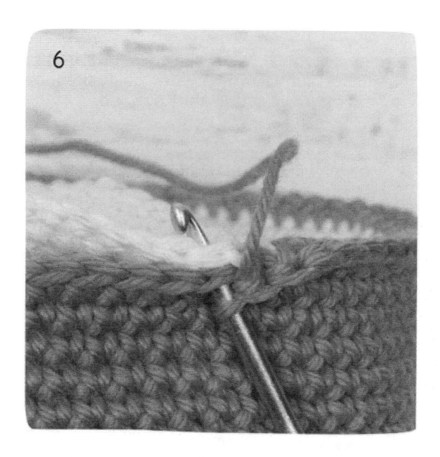

Sewing Two Pieces Together

First begin by lining up the back center of both pieces. Thread a yarn needle with the leftover yarn tail from where you fastened off or use a new length of the same color yarn from one of the pieces that you want to sew together.

Sew all around, working up and then down each stitch of both pieces, going through both loops of each stitch whenever possible, unless instructed otherwise (7 and 8). Gently pull the yarn after each stitch to make sure the pieces are securely attached and that each stitch is small and neat.

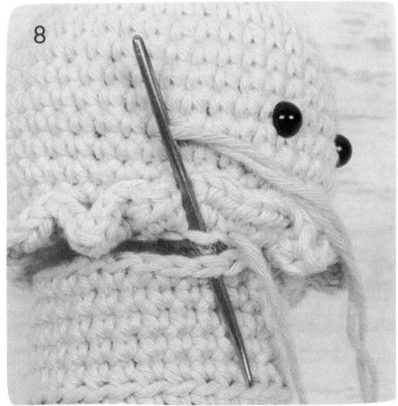

Shaping (Top Only)

Shaping makes it possible for these kawaii characters to stand up straight on a flat surface. The goal whilst shaping, unless otherwise instructed in a pattern, is to create an indentation at the bottom of the amigurumi but not at the top.

Begin shaping by inserting the needle from the center bottom of a crocheted piece to the center top (1 and 2). Insert the needle back down from the center top to slightly off the center bottom (3 and 4). Insert the needle from the center bottom to the center top (5). Pull to create an indentation in the bottom of the crochet piece (6). There should not be an indentation in the top (7). Insert the needle back down the center from the top to the bottom. Secure the yarn with two or three knots and weave in the ends.

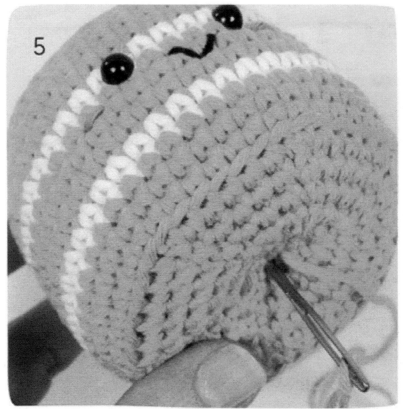

Shaping (Top and Bottom)

A few of the patterns require shaping for both the top and bottom, such as the Apple and the Pear. The end goal is to have an indentation in both the top and bottom for these amigurumi. The instructions for shaping remain the same, except when inserting the needle in and out of the top of the crocheted piece. Instead of always working in and out of the same stitch you will be working slightly off center each time so that when the yarn is gently pulled an indentation occurs.

Fastening Off Inside a Three-Dimensional Piece

With the yarn tail threaded in a yarn needle, insert the needle through the entire middle of the crochet piece. Tie a knot close to the amigurumi and push the knot inside the crocheted piece. Cut any excess yarn tail.

Stitching Facial Details

With black yarn, insert the yarn needle in the amigurumi at any point in the back and stitch on a 'V' for the mouth. The mouth should be placed in the center between the eyes and should be almost the same height as the eyes, but one round down (8 and 9).

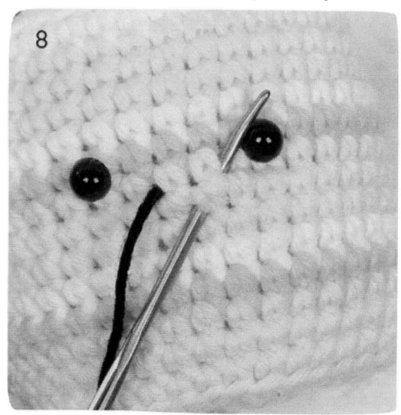

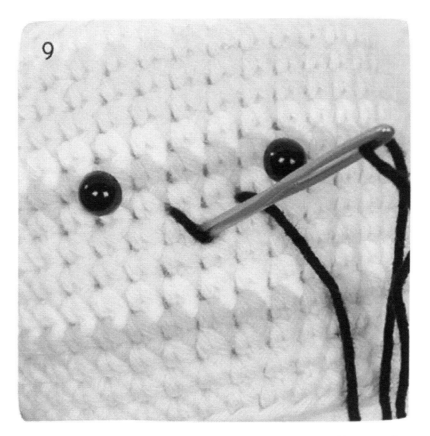

With the desired cheek color, insert the yarn needle in the amigurumi at any point in the back (10). Stitch the cheeks on either side of the eyes almost the same width as the eyes but one round down (11).

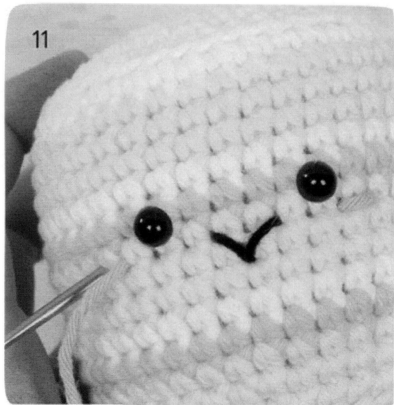

After stitching both cheeks, insert the needle through the entire middle of the crochet piece. Tie a knot close to the amigurumi and push the knot inside the crocheted piece. Cut any excess yarn tail.

When stitching on eyelashes, I find it easiest to use a double strand of sewing thread and a sewing needle. This makes it easier to work close to the safety eye and insert the needle at any point in the fabric.

Made in United States
Troutdale, OR
11/25/2024

25263602R00215